Happy Mail

A book of devotionals

Kelli Raí Collins

I dedicate this book to...

My mother, Patricia M. Robinson, who has always believed in me and has given me so much love, care and support throughout my life. Thank you for showing me what strength and love look like, Mommy. I could not have survived this life without what you have poured into my spirit.

Foreword

by Noah Washington

Have you ever felt like giving up? Has God ever seemed distant or as if He is not listening to anything that you say? Be honest, has depression become a part of your life or you just feel stressed constantly? I believe that we have all been there at some time or another. In these times of loneliness, darkness and fear it is always encouraging to have someone give you perspective. Perspective is everything! It allows you to be balanced in your understanding of life when you are erratic and life is spinning out of control.

It is important to know that through it all, God has your back and your best interest at heart. Understanding this is key because in your mind you may have lost trust in God based on your perception that He has let you down or lied to you. If you have ever struggled with your relationship with God, take courage because you are in great company. Everyone who has ever had a powerful relationship with God has struggled with their relationship with God.

When you look at heavens hall of fame recorded in Hebrews 11, it lists the names of people who have demonstrated faith in God in spite of it all. In this hall of fame are listed people who held on to God regardless of how difficult it was. What is encouraging however is the fact that the people listed there are no different from you or me. They struggled, they experienced pain, they cried, they wanted to give up; they questioned what was going on in life! I promise you, if they made it—you can make it too.

Author's Note

I started writing devotional emails in 2005 when the religious chain emails that I received from friends and coworkers seemed to be unrealistic; particularly when the email ended with instructions on how many people to forward it to and what kind of blessing or luck I'd get in return for following the instructions. These emails left me wondering what point the author was trying to convey. It seemed like sincerity was missing. Shouldn't the author just be concerned with the good message of inspiration whether or not I forwarded the message to someone else?

It made sense to me that I could spread love and encouragement to others via email, especially when God would speak to me in clear messages after I'd read a passage bible or heard a sermon or message that enlightened and uplifted me. I believe that the point of my being a Christian is to help others along life's path in whatever way God directs me to do so. There are so many people struggling, hurting, looking for clarity, and simply wanting someone to relate to from day to day. Why not be transparent and be a help to someone else? This time, I'm to help through "Happy Mail."

I have compiled the emails I've written over the years into this book after having them edited by my amazing friend, Lauri R. Preston. Each devotional email begins with "Hello Beautifuls" because that is how God sees us. We are His beautiful creation and we need to be reminded that we are "fearfully and wonderfully made" (Psalm 139:14). Each devotional ends with "Love, Kelli Raí" because I'm a willing vessel and I have sent out the message in love.

Drink the Rain

Hebrews 6:7-8 (NIV) "Land that drinks in the rain often falling on it and that produces a crop useful to those for whom it is farmed receives the blessing of God. But land that produces thorns and thistles is worthless and is in danger of being cursed. In the end it will be burned."

Hello Beautifuls,

I hope this day greeted you with wonderful warm sunshine and that you awoke with a smile. Praise God that He blesses us, and that we are blessed even more when we bask in His word and in His "Sonshine." It is up to us to keep our minds focused on Him, and hearts intact.

If you take time to read the Bible and worship daily, you will be replenished each day. If you take time to pray and meditate on Him, you will be blessed more so than when you don't spend time with him. If you fill your mind with whatever's on TV or the radio your mind will be full of that and you won't be able to experience the joy and fulfillment you have when you've taken time to worship.

I'm guilty of not having worship and time for God, as I should. But, when I *do* worship, my life has more meaning, and I hear the clear and precise answers He gives to questions I may have. I can hear Him better when I take time for Him; even my family receives a blessing from my happiness. I realize my life is not my own, and others can benefit from my relationship with God.

So today, just take some time for Him. Even if you just give Him five minutes of prayer in the car before you drive home, I'm sure you'll hunger for more. And, it's not for Him; it's for you. He wants to feed you. Don't go hungry. **Drink** from His rain that falls on you and be useful to others. Receive the blessing that is yours to claim.

Love,

Kelli Raí

The Power of Faith

1 Corinthians 4:20 (NLT) "For the Kingdom of God is not just a lot of talk; it is living by God's power."

Hello Beautifuls,

One morning I was driving my truck and there was a small bird in my path. I thought that it would surely fly away the closer I got to it, but it didn't. So I made sure that I drove right over it, centered it between my wheels, so that I wouldn't crush it. After I passed over it, I looked in my rearview mirror to find that it was fine, still in the same place. The bird didn't appear hurt or anything as I approached it, so I couldn't figure out why it didn't fly as I advanced towards it. He was unbothered as I drove away. I thought, "there must be a lesson in this." Surely I was amazed that the bird was unfazed by a large, loud, vehicle bearing down on in his direction.

Later I thought about how I'd like to be unfazed like that. I want a faith so strong and powerful that I'm not the least bit bothered when I'm faced with obstacles that I can't overcome without God's help. I want to just rely on the fact that God has never let me down; that He always comes through for me.

Recently, I re-read the book of Acts, to be reminded of the miracles that were performed once Jesus left earth. I need great miracles performed on my behalf, therefore, God has me reading, once again, about His great power and the things He has done. God has done great things through people who were faithful and willing to be used by Him. I want that kind of faith. I thirst for it. I read Acts like it's a heady novel, clinging to every word. The book is completely fascinating.

We pray to a God who can do anything. When things look hopeless, there is hope because of God's power. We should not speak as if we are hopeless. We should not act as if we are hopeless. If God can spring a well out of a dry desert, if He can form a human in a barren, post menopausal woman, if He can place Himself in human form in a virgin womb, we should be bold in our faith. Situations that are bigger than our capacity should not make us shrink; we should rely on God's power and speak boldly and move forward as we watch God perform great miracles.

I challenge you to remember that God will never leave you nor forsake you. Be bold in Him.

Love,

Kelli Raí

Judging Others

Matthew 7:1, 2a (NLT) "Stop judging others, and you will not be judged. For others will treat you as you treat them."

Hello Beautifuls,

Sometimes people take the verse, "Stop judging others and you will not be judged," only in the context of the obvious, which is: don't brow beat someone you think has done wrong. I want to take the idea a little further: don't judge from the outside what you may think is going on the inside of someone's problem. You never really know the whole story, nor do you have all the answers. Just because you *think* you have gone through something similar doesn't mean the person with the problem should do whatever you did or didn't do.

We are all unique. God has different plans and paths for each of us. He also has all the answers. It is up to the person with the issue to earnestly seek God. Your only obligation, if a person or situation has caught your attention, is to simply hold that person up in prayer. And, your prayer should not come from your own biased interpretation of what you perceive to be happening. Ask the Holy Spirit to give you the words to speak or simply ask God to move and allow His will to be done in the situation. Ask God to be in the mind of the person "going through" so they can stay sane and make the right decisions. Everything isn't always the way it seems.

There is a line in the song "Answer" by Tye Tribbett that states: "Remember not to put your trust in man, only God alone will understand what you're going through." That is a reminder of Who knows all: our Heavenly Father. Seek God and don't judge.

Love,

Kelli Rai

No Greater Love

***Psalm 9: 1-2 (KJV)** "I will praise you, O LORD, with all my heart; I will tell of all your wonders. I will be glad and rejoice in you; I will sing praise to your name, O Most High."*

Hello Beautifuls,

Today's message is all about love. A wonderful friend of mine asked me to sing with his gospel choir at church one week. The song he asked me to learn has such a beautiful message. The lyrics speak about how the blood of Jesus still holds its miraculous power!

This morning, I contemplated the words of the song and just started praising God on the way to work. I'm sure people were looking at me crazy at the stoplights, but I wasn't concerned about them; I had something to praise about!

I'm not worthy to be His child but He is my Father. I should be dead right now, but He is my Savior. In times when I feel loveless, He is my Lover. When I felt like I didn't have the right to keep on living, He comforted me and brought me through. I thank Him. I praise Him. Though I'm unworthy of His love, He loves me in spite of myself, in spite of my sin.

God allowed His only Son to come down here and die for us. He died for the sins we commit over and over and over again; the ones we can't seem to get away from. He died for the ones we plan deviously with tangled webs of lies. He died for the "little white lies." He died for our racism and prejudice and all the despicable things we do as humans. Jesus had to experience the disconnection from His divinity to become sin. He knew we would die an eternal death if He didn't sacrifice Himself, and He loved us too much to allow that to happen. For that, I cannot express my thanks enough. If I had 10,000 tongues to say "thank You", it still wouldn't be enough gratitude. I love the Lord!

Today let Him know how you feel about Him. Allow His light to shine through you. Reflect on His goodness and make a concerted effort to be pleasing to Him in your words and actions. Psalm 9: 1-2 says, "I will praise You, O LORD, with all my heart; I will tell of all Your wonders. I will be glad and rejoice in You; I will sing praise to Your name, O Most High."

Give God your praise today. Let Him know how much you love Him.

Love,

Kelli Raí

Jesus is Lord

***John 8:58 (NLT)** "Jesus answered, 'I tell you the truth, before Abraham was even born, I AM!'" ***

Hello Beautifuls,

Years ago I studied an Adult Sabbath School Bible Study Guide, entitled, "The Wonder of Jesus". One lesson in particular looked at evidence of His deity in the Bible. The question that circulated in my mind after I read it was, "who is Jesus to you?" I have had to search for the answer to that question for myself, as we all should.

That same week, I had a conversation with someone about Jesus. The person I spoke to remarked that he believed that Jesus died for all our sins but is not on God's level; that we should not make them equals. That statement amazed me. If Jesus isn't God, His dying for our sins means nothing. No being besides God can save us. The Bible points to Jesus being God and the whole doctrine of a Holy Trinity. So, somewhere along the way, some truth fell through the cracks for this brother.

Folks, if we don't search and study for ourselves we will be confused. If we ask God to guide us, He will lead us to the truth. Not **OUR** truth, **THE** truth. God is not a god of confusion; He is the God of Order. He will bring order to your chaos. You simply have to ask Him to guide you, and give you the wisdom and discernment to see truth.

I encourage you to ask yourself Who Jesus is to you, and what role He plays in your life. If you need to have a closer walk with Him along this path, open yourself to Him and take the first step by asking Him to hold your hand. Pray silently as you go about your day. Really seek and find out Who He is so that you can get to know Him better.

Love,

Kelli Raí

*Or "Before Abraham was even born, I have always been alive," The Greek reads, "Before Abraham was, I Am." (See Exodus 3:14.)

The Art of Forgiveness

Psalm 6:1 (KJV): "O LORD, rebuke me not in Thine anger, neither chasten me in Thy hot displeasure. Have mercy upon me, O LORD; for I am weak: O LORD, heal me; for my bones are vexed. My soul is also sore vexed: but Thou, O LORD, how long?"

Hello Beautifuls,

Whenever I read a passage from Psalms, I'm entertained by the drama that seems to leap from the verses. David was so passionate in his poetry and in his conversations with God. It makes me smile and helps me connect with him in a way, because I can be dramatic when I'm fearful or sad or angry. He was man after God's own heart, in spite of the sins that so easily tripped him up.

My thought for today is all about anger and working it out in the Lord. I have a problem with anger and I hold grudges. It tears me up inside from the time I am offended to the time when I can truly let go of the issue. Even if I've forgiven the person, their offense to me is ever before me when I think of them.

This is not God's design. He wants us to forgive so much that it becomes easy. He also wants us to let the issue go so much that we don't remember it. Still, God understands that we are human and it's not going to be as easy for us as it is for Him to forgive and forget. When we are in the midst of trying to forgive and striving to forget, it's alright to cry out to the Lord for help and ask Him, "How long will I agonize over this? I'm so angry I can't even function properly. Please, merciful Father, help me let go of my anger, move on and truly forgive so-and-so for doing-thus-and-so, and not remember it anymore. I want to move forward and feel good inside. I want to find my peace in You. I want to be like You."

God wants us to receive each other in love, accept each other in love, and regard each other in love, just like He does with us. The person who will be destroyed the most from anger and resentment is the person who carries it in their heart. The one against whom you are holding a grudge is probably clueless as to what is going on, especially if you already said, "I forgive you."

Ask yourself: Is it worth sleepless nights and a loss of appetite? Is it worth being consumed with anger? No, it is not. Talk to God about it, He understands. Be honest with Him and be honest with yourself. He will help you. If you have to confront the person you need to forgive, He will be your strength and your restraint (so that you do no physical harm). He is your Creator, your Father and your Confidant. He loves you and wants to show you how to live your best life.

Love,

Kelli Raí

He is with You

Genesis 31:3 (NLT) "Then the Lord said to Jacob, 'Return to the land of your father and grandfather and to your relatives there, and I will be with you.'"

Hello Beautifuls,

Genesis 31-33 is the story of Jacob returning to his father's land. God told Jacob to flee from Laban and return to the land of Canaan; that it was time to go and He would be with him.

Despite the Lord's words of comfort, "I will be with you," Jacob was still wracked with worry and stress because he would see his brother, Esau. When the two were young men, Jacob duped his brother Esau into selling his birthright and, with his mother's help, tricked his father into blessing him instead of Esau. Years later, Jacob was afraid to see Esau because he had wronged him. Jacob feared Esau – who was bigger, and the stronger of the two - would want revenge and try to take his life.

Jacob's spent that night wrestling with God, pleading for a blessing and the reassurance that God was, indeed, with him. And still, after that, he made preparations, as though he was not being protected by God; he divided up the camp in case Esau and his men were to overpower smite them, only one portion of the camp would be lost. He even divided his flocks to present as gifts to soften Esau's heart. However, Jacob need not have worried. When Esau saw him, he ran to him and hugged him. He received Jacob in joyfulness and love. Esau had let go of the past. He never intended to harm Jacob; he was simply eager to see his long lost twin brother. Had Jacob believed that God would be with him, and that no harm would come to him, he could have saved himself the worry, stress, and extra work that were unnecessarily created. In fact, Esau didn't even want to accept the gifts, but did so only because Jacob insisted.

Know that God is with us. When we seek Him for guidance and He shows the way, we should walk in that path without a care. He is our Father. He protects us, even when we don't ask for His protection. Find your comfort in God. It is not His will that we make ourselves sick with the anxiety and fear we allow to fester in our bodies. He promised to provide when we give all our burdens, all our cares to Him. If He's true (and if you don't believe, try Him), then you let go of that unhealthy relationship, you leave that job you shouldn't be working, you buy that house, you send your kids to that private school, you pay the mortgage, you pay your tithe. He's going to provide you with whatever you need to walk in the path He has laid out for you. Take to Him your cares and He will be your peace. You don't have to go through what Jacob went through. You can walk in His light, ready to receive your blessing with your head held high.

He's performing miracles every day.

Love,

Kelli Raí

Enduring Love

Psalm 117 (NLT) *"Praise the LORD, all you nations. Praise Him, all you people of the earth. For He loves us with unfailing love; the faithfulness of the LORD endures forever. Praise the LORD!"*

Hello Beautifuls,

Do you know how much the Lord loves you? Your Father loves you so much that His love is **unfailing**! No matter what you do, He loves you. No matter what you say, He loves you. No matter where you go, He loves you and His love is always with you. Even if your heart hurts so much you think you'll die from the pain, He's right there, loving you through it. His unfailing love loves you to your healing.

It's a profound moment when you can recognize unfailing love. Unfailing means, "always able to supply more; inexhaustible; constant; unflagging; incapable of error; infallible; not liable to failure; unceasing *(dictionary.com)."* To know this is the kind of love God has for me gives me reason to live. It also gives me a greater purpose, a desire to praise Him more and to strive to love Him better. I can't even imagine a love that's inexhaustible because I, as a human being, have limits. The closest thing to inexhaustible love I can think of is the love I have for my children. I also understand a love that never stops, but in my humanity, there are still strength and weakness. Nevertheless, God's love is constantly strong.

I thank God for allowing me to know His unfailing love. I can take that truth today and wrap it around my body like a warm blanket, and know that I will not suffer always. It is good for you to know, too, so that you can't ever say you are not loved. If no other human displays love for you the way you think they should, know that God's love for you is constant and it will not fail. He created you. He knew you before you were born. You were meant to be alive. Accept His unfailing love today.

Love,

Kelli Raí

Judge Rudy

Micah 7:18-20 (NIV) *"Who is a God like you, who pardons sin and forgives the transgression of the remnant of His inheritance? You do not stay angry forever but delight to show mercy. You will again have compassion on us; You will tread our sins underfoot and hurl all our iniquities into the depths of the sea."*

Hello Beautifuls,

Contrary to popular belief, God is a merciful God. He knows our hearts and our souls and He judges us accordingly. Very often we sit in the judgment seat stating things like, "so and so is going straight to hell because he or she did such and such," and "that pastor will be condemned for laying with that woman! I cannot *believe* he is back in the pulpit. I don't care if he was re-baptized."

We simply do not have any right to judge others. We don't have the right to dredge up others' shortcomings, mistakes, and sins. That's the work of Satan. He wants our sins to hold us back and keep us away from God. He wants the sins that we've repented to keep circulating in our minds to keep us from God's blessing. Sometimes we torture ourselves with the memories of our sins. But, if we've repented and turned away from those sins, God has already forgiven and forgotten. He doesn't need us to remind Him of our past sins because He hurls all our iniquities into the depths of the sea (abyss).

Let us not judge one another, but accept each other in love. When we are tempted to point out someone else's sin (current or past), let's be reminded that we are all sinners shaped in iniquity and each of us can only rely on Jesus to help us overcome. Let's help each other along life's path instead of being crabs in a barrel. Lets lift each other up instead.

God bless you!

Kelli Raí

Intercessory Prayer

Romans 8:26-27 (NIV) "In the same way, the Spirit helps us in our weakness. We do not know what we ought to pray for, but the Spirit Himself intercedes for us with groans that words cannot express. And He who searches our hearts knows the mind of the Spirit, because the Spirit intercedes for the saints in accordance with God's will."

Hello Beautifuls,

Boy, have I been struggling! A couple weeks ago, when I was almost in this same funk, I found a Bible verse that helped me. It may seem like a simple passage but when you pray it, the power of God shines brightly and you can't get away from the blessing the Holy Spirit pours out. So, I'm going to share this passage and personal prayer with you today. I hope you find a blessing in it.

"In the same way, the Spirit helps us in our weakness. We do not know what we ought to pray for, but the Spirit Himself intercedes for us with groans that words cannot express. And He's for the saints in accordance with God's will." Romans 8:26-27 NIV

Prayer: "Lord, I don't have the words to say. Please give me the right words so You can bless me; so You can save me from this pit I've fallen into. I can't see You or feel You because I've separated myself from You. Please forgive me. Please show me the way back to You. And help me to be, in some way, a blessing to someone else. In Jesus' name I pray, Amen."

If you know someone who needs you to intercede for them in prayer, please, do it today.

Love,

Kelli Raí

Favor Ain't Fair

Job 8:5-7 (NLT) "But if you pray to God and seek the favor of the Almighty, and if you are pure and live with integrity, He will surely rise up and restore your happy home. And though you started with little, you will end with much."

Hello Beautifuls,

I'd like to talk to you today about unmerited favor. Unmerited is defined as, "is not merited or deserved." Favor is defined as, "something done or granted out of goodwill, rather than from justice or for remuneration; a kind act." Unmerited favor is something that God bestows upon us. He gives it to us, not because we're so good and righteous, but because He loves us.

Unmerited favor is when you go to court, the cop doesn't show up, and your license is reinstated because your tickets have disappeared. PRAISE GOD! Unmerited favor is when your bank account looks real shady but you are blessed with trips here and there without having to worry about expenses. PRAISE GOD! Good health is unmerited favor when smoking and drinking had been a part of your social life and God gives you another chance to live a healthy life. PRAISE GOD! Unmerited favor is when you make significantly less money than your previous job but your bills are still paid and you still have enough money left over to spend on whatever else you need or want. PRAISE GOD!

Don't ever give up on prayer. Keep your communication with God open. He loves you and wants to shower you with His blessing in whatever form it comes. Favor is not always about money. Not everyone is supposed to be rich monetarily. But go to God with everything and trust Him to work out your life and He will bless you abundantly.

Love,

Kelli Raí

The Afterlife

Revelation 1:7 (KJV) "Behold, He cometh with clouds; and every eye shall see Him, and they also which pierced Him: and all kindreds of the earth shall wail because of Him. Even so, Amen."

Hello Beautifuls,

Have you heard? Jesus is coming again. His coming will seem sooner for those that die before He returns. Many people believe that when you die, you go to heaven or hell. In my personal readings of the Bible, I have not found that to be true. However, I don't look down on other people's beliefs or even debate what's true or not, I just share what I've learned. What I've learned lies in the message below.

Ecclesiastes 9:5-6 (NLT) states: *"⁵The living at least know they will die, but the dead know nothing. They have no further reward, nor are they remembered. ⁶Whatever they did in their lifetime—loving, hating, and envying—is all long gone. They no longer play a part in anything here on earth."* 1 Thessalonians 4:13-18 (KJV) states: *"¹³But I would not have you to be ignorant, brethren, concerning them which are asleep, that ye sorrow not, even as others which have no hope. ¹⁴For if we believe that Jesus died and rose again, even so them also which sleep in Jesus will God bring with Him. ¹⁵For this we say unto you by the word of the Lord, that we which are alive and remain unto the coming of the Lord shall not prevent them which are asleep. ¹⁶For the Lord Himself shall descend from heaven with a shout, with the voice of the archangel, and with the trump of God; and the dead in Christ shall rise first. ¹⁷Then we which are alive and remain shall be caught up together with them in the clouds, to meet the Lord in the air. And so shall we ever be with the Lord. ¹⁸Wherefore comfort one another with these words."*

We really need to get ready for Jesus' second coming now. We don't know exactly when He's coming and we don't know when it's our time to leave this life, so we should be ready. It's important to be very prayerful and analyze what you have been taught in church and think about what you believe. Don't just take someone's word for it; earnestly study to find answers for yourself. Seek God's wisdom and guidance. It's also a good idea to read Revelation and 1 Thessalonians 4 in your favorite bible translation (so that you understand what you are reading).

Love,

Kelli Raí

Our Protector

Psalm 91:1-4 (NLT) "Those who live in the shelter of the Most High will find rest in the shadow of the Almighty. This I declare of the LORD: He alone is my refuge, my place of safety; He is my God, and I am trusting Him. For He will rescue you from every trap and protect you from the fatal plague. He will shield you with His wings. He will shelter you with His feathers. His faithful promises are your armor and protection."

Hello Beautifuls,

I hope this bright morning finds you happy and content with life. If not, what will lift you higher is to praise God. I was listening to "You are God Alone" by Marvin Sapp over and over again one morning. The vamp of the song proclaims, "Be all Glory and Honor, Dominion and Power, Forever and Ever Amen." The words of this song lift me so high. They help me appreciate the power and the glory of God. They remind me that though I'm not worthy of His love and His presence in my life, He's taking care of me every day, every moment, and every second.

I have to give Him praise for helping me not to give in to temptations. If the only reason God exists is to keep me from things that will ruin me, it's worth it to me to accept Him. The blessing is, there is Heaven, He is coming again to take us home, He did create us, He does love us, He is on our side and He wants us to be successful. That's why Grace, Mercy, and Salvation exist.

Reflect on theme text today. Give God the praise. If your heart is hurting, give Him praise. You won't be able to stay sad when you are praising God and your face is lifted up to heaven. If you are content already, take your praise up a notch and let God carry you to the highest heights.

Love,

Kelli Raí

The Water

John 4:10 (NLT) "Jesus replied, 'If only you knew the gift God has for you and who I am, you would ask me, and I would give you living water.'"

Hello Beautifuls,

Today I encourage you to read John 4:1-4, which tells the story of Jesus talking with the Samaritan woman and ministering to her whole village for two days.

While Jesus was talking to this woman, He told her that the water He had was Living Water and if she drank it, she would never thirst again. In my imagination, I see her immediately saying, "Gimme some of that so I don't have to haul water anymore," clearly not understanding what He was really talking about. He gently went on to tell her that He wasn't speaking of physical water.

As I read that text myself, I noticed how dry my mouth was. Then I thought about why I was reading this passage and the thought occurred to me that perhaps it's because I have gotten off the path somewhat and I thirst for the relationship that I once had with God. And as I thought about it some more, noticed something - that it seemed like everything was starting to rot or go sour: from my bank account to my personal relationships. And there was nothing more I could do in my own power.

In church one Saturday, the pastor challenged us to let go of our false attachments and really try God. Now, there was no reason for my mouth to be dry when I read the text in John, because I was sitting next to a bottle of water, and I had another gallon in the car. The point is, if there are resources at hand that you know will help, but you don't use them, then things have no choice but to get bad. If you use what you know will work because it has worked in the past, it just makes sense to give it a try.

Likewise, God is within reach at all times. And even if things on the horizon look horrible, or just seem they're about to *get* horrible, He's there, on my side, to help me out come what may, OR to blow the clouds from my view so I can see what's really going on. It may not be bad at all: just a work in progress.

So, I'm gonna try Him. I encourage you to do the same. It doesn't hurt to try.

Bless you,

Kelli Raí

Robbie Knight

Philippians 1:3 (NIV) "I thank my God every time I remember you."

Hello Beautifuls,

When Robbie Knight died, my sister Lisa called to tell me. He was a college friend of hers and I would remember him because when she was in college, she used to keep me some weekends and I was around her friends. Funny, to think of it now, that the deans let an 8-9 year old stay in the college dorms on some weekends.

Anyway, when she said, "Kelli, do you remember a guy named Robbie Knight? He died in a motorcycle accident," I was shocked. I remember Robbie well. I was a little girl at the time and I thought I was ugly (despite what my parents told me on numerous occasions) and he really just made me feel special. When he first met me, he gave me the biggest smile and was so nice. Every time I saw him after that, he would give me a big hug and would hold a conversation with me as if I wasn't just an annoying little kid. I thank God for putting him in my path. He was a bright, happy spot. He made a big impact. I saw him once when I was a teenager while visiting at home on a break from school, and I haven't seen him since. The news about his passing just made me so very sad.

You never know whose life you will bless by simply being kind and friendly. You may only see certain people for a short time, but if you are intentional about making that time meaningful by allowing Jesus to shine through you, it may be such a blessing to that person. I'm sure Robbie had no idea how much of an impression he made on me, but I'll never forget him. I've been sending prayers up for his children and the rest of his loved ones. He truly was the kind of person you thank God for every time you remember him.

Love,

Kelli Raí

It's the Little Things

Matthew 6:30 (NLT) "And if God cares so wonderfully for wildflowers that are here today and thrown into the fire tomorrow, He will certainly care for you. Why do you have so little faith?"

Hello Beautifuls,

It doesn't always take a major miracle for God to show that He loves and cares for us. He does small things specifically designed just for us so that we know that He cares for our small things as well as our big things.

One morning during the time I took metro to work, I had to catch a later train than usual. The trains that came after my regular train were usually crowded and I often had to stand if I was late. Standing on the train wouldn't be so bad if I didn't suffer from motion sickness, which gets worse when I'm standing. So, I got on the train and all the seats had filled up. I walked towards the back looking around and finally stood near the door. And then God moved, just for me. A woman in the front of the train got up, turned to look at me and mouthed, "Do you want my seat?" Of course, I nodded a grateful, "Yes!" and made my way to her seat. I thanked her, thanked God and sat down and closed my eyes. God impressed upon her to give up her seat for me. I totally appreciated it because I would have been so sick if I'd had to stand up the whole way. I said a special prayer for blessings on her life.

God knows and cares about the little things that may seem small to others but mean a lot to us. He knew how tired I was that morning and He also knew what I would experience when I arrived at work, so He made my journey as smooth as possible. As I went through my stressful morning, I was constantly reminded of how He had blessed me on the train, and I was reassured that He would get me through what I needed to do that day. I stayed at ease because of how He blessed me in that very specific way.

Today, take the time to realize what God has done for you, and give Him thanks and praise. Also, be open to Him so that He can use you to bless someone else.

Love,

Kelli Raí

Don't Freak Out!

Job 42:10 (NLT) "When Job prayed for his friends, the Lord restored his fortunes. In fact, the Lord gave him twice as much as before!"

Hello Beautifuls,

Today I'd like to talk about being in distress. Having three children, I know the drama of a child calling out as if they are in distress, when, in reality, they are not. They want attention and results right away, but many times I delay and let them know that *I* know they are not truly in distress, and that they will live until I get to where they are. I can do this because I'm their parent and I know what's going on. I can see the entire situation and I know what must be done.

Sometimes, we relate to God the same way. We look at our situation and begin to worry and start praying fervently and crying. We forget that God is there, seeing the entire situation, wondering why we are trippin' because He has it all under control. He is God of all. He knows our situations and He has the solution. We have to trust Him and praise Him in the process. In fact, the Bible says we should praise Him at ALL times.

God gave us the example of Job in the Bible to show us what losing everything really means. He allowed Satan to take away all of Job's wealth and even take the lives of his children. When Satan didn't get the response he wanted from Job, God allowed him to take Job's health but not his life. Throughout this emotionally and physically painful ordeal, Job continued to give God praise and maintained his integrity as a true follower of God. For this reason, God allowed those events to take place in Job's life. God knew what His servant could handle. He knew how Job revered the Him and depended upon Him. Did God allow Job to suffer forever? No. Additionally, there is an important point for us to remember: we often reflect on what was taken away from Job, but do you remember that God restored his fortunes and gave him twice as much as he had before? In fact, He blessed him with three more daughters and seven more sons! Job went on to live 140 more years to enjoy four generations of his offspring. God restored Job with even greater blessings. PRAISE GOD!

If you are going through something now, be assured that God will not allow you to suffer through bad times forever. He is going to bless you with an even better solution because it is not His will that you suffer always. Take your bad times as character-building trials and depend wholly upon God throughout. If He allowed it, then surely He can carry you through it and give you peace in spite of how things look.

Love,

Kelli Raí

17

Testimony

Revelation 2:10-11 (NIV) "Do not be afraid of what you are about to suffer. I tell you, the devil will put some of you in prison to test you, and you will suffer persecution in ten days. Be faithful, even to the point of death, and I will give you the crown of life. He who has an ear, let him hear what the Spirit says to the churches. He who overcomes will not be hurt at all by the second death."

Hello Beautifuls,

I just want to testify about my experiences last week. Monday is when my trial started. It was a very difficult time because a friend of mine cut me off, and her reasoning didn't make any sense to me. Even though I knew I was being tested, it was nonetheless difficult for me to process. So, I prayed and attempted to be strong on my own. That's where I went wrong: I prayed but still tried to go on my own strength.

For the next couple of days I overanalyzed the issue - another bad idea, since I should have just given it to God and let it go. Anyway, I decided to fast on Thursday. I felt weak physically, emotionally, and spiritually but I fasted anyway because I knew I needed to. I was weary the whole day and felt especially heavy near the end of my fast. I read Romans 8 and found strength in God's promises there, and I prayed and praised God. The Holy Spirit guided me through my prayer and urged me to give my sadness, anger, and weakness to God. Afterwards, I was surprised that I felt happy. I thought I was going to carry my sadness way into the evening, even at my rehearsal, but I left my burden with God and He took it from me. I was smiling and happy at the end of that fast.

For confirmation that God's got my back, the sermon I heard on Sabbath ("No Pain, No Gain") was about being strengthened through trials, tribulation, and suffering. The church of Smyrna, which was characterized by trials, tribulation, and suffering in that day, still thrives because of it. Smyrna continually rebuilt itself after being ravaged by war and earthquakes. The take-home message is that if you have Jesus with you and *in* you, you don't have to worry because He's never going to leave you. Even if you die, He will raise you up at the Second Coming. And when trials come, there is a way to deal with them positively rather than wallow in the resulting pain. Ask Jesus to help you deal with these situations differently. He *will* help you; I am a witness to that. He will show up when you need Him to show up!

God is always in control. We can have confidence that He wants us to grow in Him and be strong. We gain strength by tests and trials but through it all, He will be there to show us the way to Him. So, rely on His strength, as His return gets closer. He loves you. He really does.

Love,

Kelli Raí

The Spirit of Fear

2 Kings 19:2, 3 (NLT) *"So Jezebel sent this message to Elijah: 'May the gods strike me and even kill me if by this time tomorrow I have not killed you just as you killed them.' Elijah was afraid and fled for his life. He went to Beersheba, a town in Judah, and he left his servant there."*

Hello Beautifuls,

There are times when we experience fear in our lives because of various circumstances we face. The only reason why we truly get scared is because we have not reminded ourselves of God's faithfulness. God may have recently done something mighty in our own lives or someone close to us but with the new situation, our memory has fails us.

It's not God's plan for us to live in fear. It's not God's will for us to live without His goodness and His unfailing love. In the theme verse, Elijah had *just* experienced God's power. He showed the people of Israel that God is Lord of all by presenting a very wet sacrifice that the Lord engulfed in flames from Heaven. But when the demonic queen Jezebel threatened his life, he became afraid and fled. How quickly he forgot that God is God of all and would spare his life! When Elijah came to his senses, God revealed Himself to him. God told him to prophesy new leaders into existence, and an apprentice for himself. He also instructed Elijah to prophesy Jezebel's gory death, just to prove that God had his back.

Sometimes, it's hard to believe that God is really on your side because things don't seem to get better. Or maybe as soon as something gets better, you're blindsided with something else. Whatever the case, you have to appeal to God for His mercy, grace and peace. Sometimes you're required to fast and pray for a time. Sometimes God calls you to rely solely on Him to increase your faith. Regardless, He always comes through. If you ask, He will guide you to do exactly what you must do. It's up to you to be open to Him and do what He tells you to do. Some of the lessons you learn in life are just for you. Other lessons you learn are for you to share with others so that their faith can grow.

Be open to Him. It will get better.

Love,

Kelli Raí

He Loves Us

Job 10:12 (NLT) "You gave me life and showed me Your unfailing love. My life was preserved by Your care."

Hello Beautifuls,

This morning on my way into work, I was thinking about God's wonderful love for me. I know that He loved all of us so much that He sent Jesus down from beautiful Heaven to this slum, Earth, to save our lives. That, however, was not my focus. I was thinking about how He stepped in and was my Father where my father fell short and stepped in as my Mother when my mother fell short. I didn't have a horrible upbringing, but it wasn't perfect - and I don't know anyone who has had a perfect upbringing. God filled in the gaps that needed to be filled to make me the woman I am today.

My thoughts of God's love reached even to when I was broken as a young college girl, and God built me back up. He loved me and didn't want me to die so He saved my life. And later, in these recent years, He loved my husband, children, and me so much that He took chaos out of my household and put everything in order. With the order He placed in my household, He has blessed others. Remember, our lives are not our own and the things you do have an effect on other people. Case in point: a woman at church was sending up Hallelujahs this past Sabbath for my marriage and the blessing it has been to her! I haven't ever been this happy or satisfied before in my adult life. I give God all the glory and honor and praise and adulation! I give Him my life. I give Him my voice. I give Him me, Kelli, to use as He sees fit for His glory.

God has blessed me with wonderful family members, friends, and colleagues. I'm blessed beyond what I can hold. My cup literally overflows. My heart is filled, so I must share it with all of you. I hope you can feel the love I'm praying your way today. I hope you can look back on this year and see it as the Best Ever. And I hope next year is even better than this.

Love and blessings,

Kelli Raí

He Knows Our Struggles

Matthew 26:39 (NLT) "He went on a little farther and bowed with His face to the ground, praying, 'My Father! If it is possible, let this cup of suffering be taken away from Me. Yet I want Your will to be done, not Mine.'"

Hello Beautifuls,

I am sitting here, listening to some music - getting a "gospel boost" - and I simply had to testify to how much God loves us. The Sabbath school lesson this week spoke of the last few days of Jesus' life and how, in the Garden of Gethsemane, He struggled in His human nature. His Spirit was willing to finish His work here on earth, but His flesh was weak. Jesus had to pray and cry out to God, even though He ultimately knew what God's will was. *(See Matthew 26:36-44)*

That passage is significant because it demonstrates how Jesus can truly understand when we struggle with our own human inclinations. He knows what we go through, having been "born a sinner" (Psalm 51:5). It is comforting to know that when I fall on my knees to repent, or ask Him for answers or simply plead with Him, He understands. His life also demonstrated that we humans could live a sin-free life, through **His** strength, just as He did through His Father's strength. When He says, "go and sin no more" we can, because He is our example (John 8:11).

Praise God for Jesus' decision to die on the cross for our sins! I thank Him for not giving into His flesh and deciding to save us even when we He knew we would turn our backs on Him time and time again. If we were to look to Him daily for guidance and as our example, just think how enriched our lives would be! Even through trials, struggles, and hard times, we can think, "You know, Jesus knows exactly what this is and He can help me through this. His might and power can deliver me from this pain or situation or destructive pattern." Thank God we have this promise manifest in our Savior.

The more we praise Him, the more we realize His power and love for us. In the coming days, let's spend more of our time praising God and counting our blessings.

God bless you.

Love,

Kelli Raí

Poem of Forgiveness

Psalm 79:9 (NLT) "Help us, O God of our salvation! Help us for the honor of Your name. Oh, save us and forgive our sins for the sake of Your name.

Your holy hands
molded my body into being
blessed the union of my parents
formed my eyes, ears, mouth, hands, feet, heart, soul...
only by Your mercy am I complete

Your holy arms
hold me in comfort's bliss
whenever I'm in pain or seeking peace
protect me from ruin

Your omniscient mind
knows my every thought
my comings and goings... my iniquity
yet still has the capacity to love and forgive me

I humbly bow before You
boldly requesting Your forgiveness
asking that I be restored back inside Your fold
so that I am free to be free in You
again....

- Kelli Raí

God's Message to Me

Romans 8:28 (NLT) "And we know that God causes everything to work together for the good of those who love God and are called according to His purpose for them."

Hello Beautifuls,

In church one Sabbath, the speaker had us turn in our bibles to Romans 8:9-12 and after I turned there I noticed a note that I had written on the next page. It had verses 26-28 underlined and the note said "3.10.07 God's msg to me." I got chills when I saw that note.

Verses 26 and 27 speak about how the Holy Spirit helps us in our weakness, even going as far as to intercede for us when we don't know what to pray. (This happens to me more often than not: the "not knowing" what to say in prayer.) When the Holy Spirit intercedes on our behalf, God listens and understands because He knows our hearts, and the Spirit pleads for us in harmony with God's own will. Then it comes down to God causing everything to work together for the good of those who love Him! Praise God!

Previously, I wrote about God truly knowing our hearts. This passage in Romans 8 shows that, even with knowing our true hearts (the good and bad of it), the Holy Spirit steps in on our behalf to the Father *anyway*. This proves that He loves us and wants the best for us, even if we keep making poor choices. Throughout His word, God continually shows us His love, mercy and grace.

When I think of some the trials I have experienced, I realize how both the good and the bad times worked together for my good. I was able to witness and testify to God's keeping on every occasion. I now see how God used me in spite of myself to bless others. And when God uses me, it is a blessing and a humbling experience.

Today, take stock of your relationship with God. Has it grown? Has it dwindled? Read the passages I mentioned today, and trust God.

He is always there for you.

Love,

Kelli Raí

You are Worthy of Forgiveness

Psalm 103:8-14 (NLT) "The Lord is compassionate and merciful, slow to get angry and filled with unfailing love. He will not constantly accuse us, nor remain angry forever. He does not punish us for all our sins; He does not deal harshly with us, as we deserve. For His unfailing love toward those who fear Him is as great as the height of the Heavens above the earth. He has removed our sins as far from us as the east is from the west. The Lord is like a father to His children, tender and compassionate to those who fear Him. For He knows how weak we are; He remembers we are only dust."

Hello Beautifuls,

Recently, God reminded me of His character. At the time, I was feeling down, unlovable, and unforgivable. I was feeling like the prodigal son felt when he was eating slop in the pigpen. On top of that, the devil was doing a number on me, telling me how undeserving and terrible I am, and how I shouldn't even ask God for forgiveness for anything I'd done. God saw all that the devil was trying to do, but I didn't call on Him. It was a pretty emotionally trying day for me.

That evening, during family worship, the children decided they wanted to read passages from the Bible. When I opened the Bible to read after they had finished, I silently asked God to guide me to a passage. He led me to Psalm 103. I don't know why I didn't just shout and dance then! In that moment, He spoke directly to me through His word, and reminded me He loves me in spite of myself. See, God doesn't treat us how we treat each other. He doesn't even give us the punishment we deserve. He is forgiving, loving, compassionate, all knowing, all seeing, merciful, and kind.

Beautifuls, God loves you! He loves you far beyond anything you can fathom. He will forgive you if you ask. He then chooses to forget your confessed sin and won't ever bring it up again. He does not cause guilt or shame; that's not His style. Don't let anyone tear you down. Keep on persevering through this life. Admit your mistakes, and move on; just try not to do them again. Give your cares to God.

He's there, waiting to commune with you.

Love,

Kelli Raí

When You Stop Worrying…

Matthew 6:31-32 (NLT) "So don't worry about these things saying, 'What will we eat? What will we drink? What will we wear?' These things dominate the mind of unbelievers, but your Heavenly Father already knows all your needs. Seek the Kingdom of God above all else, and live righteously, and He will give you everything you need."

Hello Beautifuls,

God blessed me with that verse above on February 16, 2008. It was His message to me because I was worried about money and how we were going to maintain our bills since I had been laid off and had just received my last paycheck. I didn't know when I was going to get another steady job that paid what my last job paid. And though I intellectually know God provides for my family and me, I found myself worrying because I like to have an idea of what to expect and I had no clue what was going to happen next.

Well! God provided a job for me at the kids' school (which they were excited about) and it paid enough. God then blessed us with enormous checks we weren't expecting so we could pay bills and get our car fixed. He went all out for us because I decided to stop worrying and keep on giving my job opportunities to Him, asking Him to take care of our finances. He went above and beyond what I expected.

I am in praise mode. Not just because of what He's done but because of what He's continuing to do in my life. He constantly shows up and blesses me beyond anything I can imagine. It's not because I deserve it or because I'm the best Christian ever (I'm not). It's just because He loves me, and wants to see my family thrive and be successful. He wants that for all His children.

Increase your faith today. Trust that the Lord will provide all your needs no matter what your outlook may be at this moment. He has not brought you this far just for you to fall apart. He has success and blessings for you.

Love,

Kelli Raí

It's Not About You

Psalm 8 (NIV): "O LORD, our Lord, how majestic is Your name in all the earth! You have set Your glory above the Heavens. From the lips of children and infants You have ordained praise because of Your enemies to silence the foe and the avenger. When I consider Your Heavens, the work of Your fingers, the moon and the stars, which You have set in place, what is man that You are mindful of him, the son of man that You care for him? You made him a little lower than the Heavenly beings and crowned him with glory and honor. You made him ruler over the works of Your hands; You put everything under his feet: all flocks and herds, and the beasts of the field, the birds of the air, and the fish of the sea, all that swim the paths of the seas. O LORD, our Lord, how majestic is Your name in all the earth!"

Hello Beautifuls,

Night before last, I had trouble sleeping and couldn't figure out why. It could have been because I was rehearsing a song I arranged and I was on a natural high. It could have been because God wanted to talk to me. Whatever the case, I got out of bed, decorated some cupcakes for Zoie and washed the dishes. As I was washing the dishes (at 1 am), I thought of something I used to say all the time when I was a new mother, "It's not about you; it's all about how God uses you to help someone else. It's not about you!" I believe this phrase came to mind because I have a habit of putting limits on how God can possibly use me for His service. And I put limits on His blessings for me. I have to be reminded that He's in control.

That message had been realized earlier that night at rehearsal. I suggested to the musicians there getting a band together since I wanted to do a concert in the summer. They didn't laugh or look at me all crazy, just said, "Oh sure, definitely." I was floored. I saw that someone outside of my circle thought I have enough talent to do a solo concert and was willing to help me make it happen. That's God. That's God having more confidence in me than I have in myself. God sings through me and flows through the lyrics I write for Him to touch others. Praise God! Hallelujah! I thank Him for using me.

God wants to use us to help each other along life's path. Make yourself available to Him. It can be an encouraging word. It can be a smile someone needs to see in passing. It can be a warm hug to a friend. You never know what's happening in someone else's life, so make yourself available to God daily. It's not all about you, and the passage today is what I share with you as praise to God.

I'm so thankful that God reminded me once again that it's not all about me: it's about Him. Ponder that a while.

Love,

Kelli Raí

My God is So High

Ephesians 3:18-19 (NLT) *"And may you have power to understand, as all God's people should, how wide, how long, how high, and how deep His love is. May you experience the love of Christ, though it is too great to understand fully. Then you will be made complete with all the fullness of life and power that comes from God."*

Hello Beautifuls,

Sometimes it's difficult to accept God's love because we think that we don't deserve it. And honestly, we don't deserve it because He knows our hearts. When we use the phrase "God knows our hearts or my heart," we're using it to say we're pretty good on the inside. I challenge you: take an *honest* look at yourself. God *knows* your heart. He knows when you're faking. He knows when you're going through the motions. He knows how you really feel about that person at church or person at work or family member that you can't stand. He knows when you lust after that person you shouldn't be lusting after in your mind. He knows how you plopped out the food on your family's plates because you were in a bad mood and didn't feel like parenting or "adulting." He knows about that good thing you decided to do which really was just about bringing attention to yourself. He knows you, and He loves you in spite of who you really are.

Paul was aware of God's love and he knew that we humans could never really understand "how wide, how long, how high, and how deep" God's love is for us. His love is all of those things: wider, longer, higher and deeper than we could ever conceptualize. I don't even really try to understand God's love. I work on just accepting it because I want to receive from Him everything He has for me. He has blessed me so far beyond what I ever expected. I asked Him to bless me and, true to His promises, He has done so.

God loves us so much that He sent Jesus to die for us though we are ungrateful. Jesus suffered on the cross for our sins though we live as if we can't stop sinning. We'll never be able to fully understand God's love but we should work on drawing close to Him. We need to love Him with all our might and receive all that He has for us. We need to make time for Him because when we draw nigh to Him, He'll draw nigh to us.

Love,

Kelli Raí

Don't Stop! Don't Give Up!

Matthew 7:7-8 (NLT) "Keep on asking, and you will be given what you ask for. Keep on looking, and you will find. Keep on knocking and the door will be opened. For everyone who asks, receives. Everyone who seeks, finds. And the door is opened to everyone who knocks."

Hello Beautifuls,

There comes a time in everyone's life when you want to give up on praying because it doesn't seem to work, or you're mad at God for some reason, or you get too busy with your life, etc. Whatever the reason is, you shouldn't give up on prayer. My father once told me when I was in college, "No matter where you are in your life, no matter what you are doing, God always wants to hear from you. You can always pray." Taking his advice [much later] I discovered that even if I was in places I should not have been, or done things I should not have done, or even said things I should have never said, when I prayed, God still listened. God still communed with me. In spite of all the junk I put in my life, He always finds me and manages to bring me out of my clutter.

One day when I was praying, I asked God to come in and cleanse me. I told Him I was willing to be used by Him no matter what. I asked Him to reveal my purpose and use me to save someone else's life. After that, God kept reminding me of my request. Even when I brought clutter back into my world from time to time, He kept using me. More and more, I meet people who are crying out for God but they don't know how to rely on Him, or they're in desperate need of His comfort but they don't have the words to say, or they're simply out of touch. He's putting these people in my path so that I can pray for them and give an encouraging word, without being all "religious" and in their face about what they should or shouldn't be doing. As He reveals my purpose and uses me, He blesses me, strengthens me, and prepares me for what He has in store.

Beautifuls, prayer is real and it works. It is a true gift and a privilege to be able to commune with God. We don't have to even move our lips. We can simply talk to Him from our heart. And it doesn't have to be all elaborate and eloquent. There have been times I didn't have the words to say and I just said to Him, "Save me, Lord. Please help me and save me." I'm still here in my right mind [that means a lot, because mental illness runs in my family]. I have strength and our Creator blesses me. It's also wonderful to pray for someone who can't pray for him or herself. You never know how your prayer for someone else can change a life or situation. I am a witness.

Don't stop talking to God. He wants to hear from you. Matt 6:30 (NLT) says, "And if God cares so wonderfully for flowers that are here today and gone tomorrow, won't he more surely care for you...." Keep asking. Keep seeking. Keep knocking.

Love,

Kelli Raí

The Art of Not Listening

Psalm 121:2 (NLT) "My help comes from the Lord, who made heaven and earth!"
Psalm 124:8 (NLT) "Our help is from the Lord, who made heaven and earth."

Hello Beautifuls,

When we ask God to increase our faith or patience or some other virtue we need help in developing, He will do it in a way we don't expect. He gives lessons, tests, and trials to work the "muscle" that needs strengthening. It can be a very humbling experience when God is doing for us exactly what we ask. Sometimes we have to step back to realize what is really going on.

One evening, I was feeling melancholy for no particular reason. I was home by myself and didn't really have anything that I needed to do. God whispered, "This is a perfect opportunity for us to spend some time together." Ignoring this suggestion, I decided to go to my cousin's house. God said, "You need to stay home." I did not stay home. Leaving the driveway, my gaslight came on. I drove past my cousin's house to get gas. The gas tank would not accept my card. (I knew I had enough money to get gas but it would not allow me to pump.) While fuming, I got a text from my friend who had Solomon saying that she would be at my house in 15-20 minutes. I could not go to my cousin's house and had to go back home. I pulled over and moved money around in my bank account so that I could get gas at the next station. God whispered, "Do not get gas tonight, just go home and stay there."

I met Solomon at home and after he was in the house I went to another gas station to get gas. I STILL could not get gas! The money transfer registered but didn't register. Then I thought, "God did say to go home. I'm totally being disobedient." I went home and sat down in my living room, opened the bible to Psalm 121 then I read the surrounding chapters. I noticed that Psalm 121:2 and Psalm 121:8 stood out because they were so similar. I did a search online and found that these are the only two verses that relate God helping and the fact that He is the Creator. The message to me was this: God is the maker of heaven and earth and He is equipped to help me. He wanted to help me the whole time. He wanted me to sit still and give my weight of melancholy to Him. He wanted to be my company, my peace. After conversing about this with my brother, I got on my knees to pray and asked God for forgiveness and thanked Him and asked Him to continue to help my faith and continue cover my finances.

The next morning I was able to get gas. My husband moved more money around but even if he hadn't; I still would have been able to get gas. God was holding up that progress last night to get my attention, because the money was there.

I am so thankful that I worship a God who cares enough to be actively involved in my spiritual development. We are not to do everything on our own, we are to ask for guidance and allow God to lead us and to LISTEN to Him when He is leading.

My challenge for you is to spend more time communicating with God: listen more.

Love,

Kelli Raí

Rock the Boat

1 Peter 5:8-9 (NLT) "Stay alert! Watch out for your great enemy, the devil. He prowls around like a roaring lion, looking for someone to devour. Stand firm against him, and be strong in your faith. Remember that your Christian brothers and sisters all over the world are going through the same kind of suffering you are."

Hello Beautifuls,

Most times when I hear people say that they get up early in the morning to read the Bible and pray, and they carry their Bibles with them all the time, I think that maybe they're fanatics. Ok, so I don't always wake up and first thing flip open my Bible. But I should. And I started today. The Bible says that we must, "Stay alert! Watch out for your great enemy, the devil. He prowls around like a roaring lion, looking for someone to devour. Stand firm against him, and be strong in your faith." It's true that our **enemy** the devil is aiming to destroy us. How can we stay alert and watch out if we don't take time for personal worship? How can we be strong in our faith if we're not in touch with our **Ally,** our **Creator,** and our **Father**?

Last week, God told me to encourage this man that I was sitting next to on the bus. I told Him no. And I didn't know why He wanted to use me because I hadn't really prayed that day nor had I studied His Word. I wondered, "Why He would You use me, of all people?" Still, the Spirit urged me to say something to encourage this man before I got to my stop. I noticed that he held a job listing in his hand, and he was sweating on an air-conditioned bus. I knew I had better say something. As I was getting up to leave, I touched his arm and said, "Stay optimistic." He said, "What?" I had to say it twice, and then I said, "Your hope? Keep it up!" He finally understood and said "Thank you!" His face lit up and he waved to me as the bus pulled off. Now, perhaps if I had spoken to him the first time God told me to, I wouldn't have gotten flustered so he couldn't understand me, and he might have smiled longer. He definitely would have been encouraged sooner. I'm glad that God used me to keep this man's hope alive. Sometimes, when I don't do my part in seeking His face in worship, I feel unprepared when He wants to use me.

Even after that humbling experience, I still didn't learn my lesson and the devil tripped me up, so that now I'm in a "pit." But yesterday, I was ministered to and told that when you're in a pit, make it your prayer closet and the angels will minister to you. It is also where you get one on one time with the Lord. So, I am encouraged that in the midst of mistakes made, God will build you [me] up again. If you stay faithful, you will be stronger and more ready for arrows thrown at you. You will also realize that God is your strength and will keep you alert!

Stay strong in the Lord, you Beautifuls.

Love,

Kelli Raí

Summations

Jeremiah 15:19 (NLT) "This is how the Lord responds: 'If you return to me, I will restore you so you can continue to serve me. If you speak good words rather than worthless ones, you will be my spokesman. You must influence them; do not let them influence you!'"

it's amazing how we sum up people in a few short words:
       "she's a good mom"
       "she's short with a classic bob"
       "she's a housewife"
       "he's a dedicated worker,"
totally taking away from the depth of who they really are
       "she's a good mom" really means,
       "she is so dedicated to her children that she sacrifices her own wants so they can live a full life and have the best education."
we spend so much time summing people up,
it takes away from what they truly mean to us
we even do it to God
we throw around "God is love"
when we should say
"God is my all... is in every breath I take... saves my life everyday... gives me hope upon hope for tomorrow."
we need to start being lengthy when speaking about others...
especially when we love them and they mean so much to us
my husband is not just a good man
he sacrifices all the time to provide for his family... is such a part of me that I speak his thoughts
and I... I am not just regular... am very special and constantly embark upon and complete some very extraordinary endeavors
we should make it a habit to tell people how much they mean to us...
tomorrow is not promised
and words... they depth of words have the potential to save lives...
words created the universe... you and me...
make a commitment to say more and mean it.

-Kelli Raí

Praise God!

Romans 4:20 (NLT) "Abraham never wavered in believing God's promise. In fact, his faith grew stronger, and in this he brought glory to God."

Hello Beautifuls,

I just want to take some time out to give God praise. I was listening to "Sinking" on Tye Tribbett & G.A.'s cd *Victory Live*. I've heard this song a million times but yesterday, as it did the first time I heard it, the words moved me to tears:

> "When I think of the goodness of Jesus and all He has done for me; my soul cries out HALLELUJAH! Thank God for saving me! I was sinking so deep in sin and so very deeply stained within but God, oh, but God! He's been good!"

Have you ever been so caught up in a sin that you knew you couldn't save yourself? That it would take Divine Power to pull you out? I've been there, more than once. And I thank God for pulling me out of my cycle of self-destruction. I praise God from Whom all blessings flow, Who gives us brand new mercy with each dawning!

Now, you don't have to praise God by shouting or jumping or crying, but like Abraham, simply "believe in God's promise," as it says in today's verse. Grow in your faith! Trust Him! Trust in His Word! Look to Him for guidance! Be confident that He will do what He says He will do. He saved me! Some folks think that I became a Christian just because my father was a preacher. My, my! The stories he could have told about my rebellion! However, I had to find my way. I had to allow God to take me outside of denomination-mindedness and lead me to **Christianity**.

So many of us caught up in being pious and Pharisaic that we don't even see ourselves anymore as Christians being lights to others, helping others live better lives. No, we turn God off to others with our "don't wear this, don't eat that, don't listen to that, and oh, you saw *what* movie?" COME ON! Be an example of how you should live, don't bark demands! Did Jesus turn up His nose at the people who needed Him? No. He saved them. I PRAISE GOD because He loves me more than I'll ever realize. And He SO loves you too!

Take out some time today to reflect on God's promises, His goodness and mercy towards you. He just wants to commune with you one more time.

Love,

Kelli Raí

Rejoice with Me!

Romans 12:15 (NLT) "Be happy with those who are happy, and weep with those who weep."

Hello Beautifuls,

Today I invite you to be happy with me like the verse above says. I am so full of happiness and a feeling like this can only come from God above. He has blessed me so extensively recently. [He always blesses but He went all out to show me His love this past week.]

First of all, I did the master-cleansing fast for nine days, a great feat for me because I adore food. God gave me the strength and stamina to push through the hard days and I lost 11 pounds as a result. Second, we are getting a check for our damaged van, which will be for a greater monetary amount than we thought. Third, I keep getting opportunities to minister for Him by singing and testifying. This joy that I have couldn't be snatched away in this moment. I invite you now, to glorify God with me. He is so good. As I've said countless times before, I don't deserve any good thing from Him, but He blesses me in spite of myself. And now, I shower Him with my love. I love Him so much! He goes all out for His rebellious daughter and I praise His name.

Take time today to think on something He' done for you, even today's blessing, and just close your eyes and thank Him. Now that my eyes are misting up, I'll end this message.

Praise God from Whom all blessings flow;
Praise Him all creatures here below;
Praise Him above, ye Heavenly hosts;
Praise Father, Son, and Holy Ghost!

Love,

Kelli Raí

Protection

2 Samuel 22:3 (NLT) "My God is my rock, in whom I find protection. He is my shield, the power that saves me, and my place of safety. He is my refuge, my Savior, the One who saves me from violence."

Hello Beautifuls,

You know, most of the time we are shielded from the dangers that God protects us from, but sometimes we are made aware of how we've been kept safe. Last night I was made aware that God is "my Savior, the one who saves me from violence." Long story short, someone had road rage, yelled at me and threw something metal at my car. Now, I say, "threw something metal" because it sounded like something metal hit the car I was driving. I slammed on my brakes and let them go on. My heart racing and I was frightened, but God immediately told me that He protected me from danger.

As I continued my journey home, the scene replayed in my mind, and I realized I could have been hurt because my window was open, but God was my personal Force Field. I can't thank Him enough. He saved me from being a morning news story. I prayed in the car and prayed at home. After I parked in my driveway, I looked at the driver's side of the car (in the darkness) and didn't see any scrapes or anything. I checked again this morning and still saw nothing; that compounded the reality of God's protection.

Dorinda Clark-Cole sings a song called "Nobody But God" and the vamp always moves me to tears. It definitely did this morning; "Nobody did it, but God." Only God can foresee any danger and be your shield, your power, your safety, your refuge, and your Savior from danger. I thank Him. Take some time out today to thank God for keeping you safe from dangers seen and unseen.

Love,

Kelli Raí

God is on Our Side

Psalm 56:3, 4, 8-10 (NLT) "But when I am afraid, I put my trust in You. O God, I praise Your Word. I trust in God, so why should I be afraid? What can mere mortals do to me?" (v 8-10) "You keep track of all my sorrows. You have collected all my tears in Your bottle. You have recorded each one in Your book. On the very day I call to You for help, my enemies will retreat. This I know: God is on my side. O God, I praise Your Word. Yes, LORD, I praise Your Word."

Hello Beautifuls,

We don't have to stress, be worried, or be afraid of anything at any time. God is on our side. It's not just a cliché; it's there in His Word. He keeps track of all our sorrows. What we have to work on is giving our cares and worries to Him, and leaving them there.

My pastor once preached that it is a sin to give your problems over to the Lord and pick them back up again to try and fix things ourselves. If we believe that God is all knowing, then we shouldn't worry that things won't work out in good time. We have to trust Him to work it out. I know it's difficult but I tried it for myself. I immediately felt relief that I could give my problems away to God. And when I stressed again five minutes later, I was reminded that I had picked it up again.

We make such a mess of things when we try to fix things that are out of our control. If our hands are tied and nothing more can be done, stressing about it does not help anything. It is far better to let go of the issue and have a peace about it; giving the issue to God as many times as we begin to worry about it again. He is on our side.

Love,

Kelli Raí

Giving Up to Allow Change

Psalm 23:4 (NLT) "Even when I walk through the darkest valley, I will not be afraid, for you are close beside me. Your rod and your staff protect and comfort me."

Hello Beautifuls,

Today the thought is about giving up on the people you love. Recently, I judged someone close to me for giving up on her loved one because of the detrimental choices he's made. It seemed unbelievable to give up on someone you really love. Why would you do that? Then God put me in my place and let me know that it can be a divine thing that God ordains when someone gives up on you, or when you give up on someone. He reminded me of the time a close friend of mine gave up on her marriage because she was tired of the pain she and her husband had put each other through for years. She gave up on her husband because she felt that he would never change. It was God that took her to that place. Together, they put the marriage in God's hands and now their marriage is stronger than ever. God took them through that valley. God showed both of them that change could come, through Him and by His Divine power.

Sometimes God has to lead us through valleys so that we can appreciate the mountaintop. Some people have to believe that they are really alone in a lifeless valley before they finally give God a try. If you know someone who's gone through life learning the hard way, and they seem to continue on that path, pray for them. And if you know someone who's had to give up on someone for their own peace of mind, pray for them, also. There's nothing like intercessory prayer. Maybe God has put you in the situation or "in the know" so that you can go before Him on their behalf.

You know the saying: "God works in mysterious ways." Well, they're really not mysterious. He knows all and He has a method to salvation.

Love,

Kelli Raí

Just Pray

Ezra 9:6 (NLT): I prayed, "Oh my God, I am utterly ashamed; I blush to lift up my face to you. For our sins are piled higher than our heads, and our guilt has reached to the Heavens."

Hello Beautifuls,

This morning, I woke up with the song, "Second Chance" by Hezekiah Walker playing in my mind: "You gave me a second chance/ You forgave me like only you can/ You gave me a second chance!" The Lord kissed me with that song this morning to let me know that I can start fresh today.

Last week was rough. It seemed that the more into the week I got, the further from God I got. I was hardly in communion with Him at all. My most stressful day was Friday. I was emotional and had not allowed God to take care of me, even though the morning before He awoke me with another song: "Give it to Me, I'll bear it... give it to Me, I'll share it... if there's a need in your life, I will take it if you only give it to Me" (James Cleveland "Give it to Me"). I ignored His offer. That evening, I watched Praise The Lord with CeCe Winans as host. The theme was prayer. My "I can take care of myself" attitude was broken when they began talking about intercessory prayer. At that point I asked myself, "How can I be about God at all times?" The answer is what I already know: time, prayer, worship, and praise. I apologized to God for turning my back to him. He answered with giving me another chance.

When you don't feel like praying (for yourself or anyone else), do it anyway. God will take it from there. He just wants to spend time with you. You may find yourself forgetting about anything else that may be on your mind because prayer has taken you to a completely different space. Let God take you to a place of safety, to a place where you don't have a worry, to a place where you can just be alone with Him.

He really loves you.

Love,

Kelli Raí

The Power of Words

John 1:1-4 (KJV) "In the beginning was the Word, and the Word was with God, and the Word was God. He was in the beginning with God. All things were made through Him, and without Him nothing was made that was made. In Him was life, and the life was the light of men."

Hello Beautifuls,

Today's passage is referring to Jesus as the Word of God. Jesus spoke all of His creations into being. He wasn't required to speak - I'm sure He could have created everything quietly - but He spoke and his creations came to be. To me, this is such a powerful demonstration of the power words can have. No, we are not as omnipotent like God is, but He gave us the power to speak, to use our minds to choose our words. This is why the words we allow to come out of our mouths are important. God delighted in David because he used his words to praise God in poetry and in song. God inhabits our praise because it is positive and true, building Him up and telling others of His greatness. We need to praise Him in our daily lives, but also speak words of positivity and truth to and about others so they, too, can experience God's love.

At times we don't recognize the power of words. Words can destroy just as easily as they build up a person. Speaking words of truth and positivity not only builds up the person to whom they're directed (especially our children) but also builds your own character and enriches your own life. Letting someone know you think they are a good person, or that you appreciate something they did for you can be the encouragement they need to carry on. Many of us smile on the outside while bitterly struggling on the inside. We all benefit from hearing something good to keep us going.

Today, take the time to be that smiling, positive, encouraging voice to someone, anyone. You could be saving someone's life.

Love,

Kelli Raí

Faith like Hannah's

Samuel 2:1-2 (NLT) Then Hannah prayed: "My heart rejoices in the Lord! Oh, how the LORD has blessed me! Now I have an answer for my enemies, as I delight in your deliverance. No one is holy like the LORD! There is no one besides you: there is no Rock like our God...."

Hello Beautifuls,

Today, I want to talk about God's power. Our God is all-powerful. In 1 Samuel 2, Samuel's mother Hannah, sent a prayer to God, praising Him for blessing her barren womb with a son, whom she dedicated to Him. God delivered her from the despair she endured for years, being taunted by her husband's other wife Penninah; Penninah had many children while Hannah had none. God blessed Hannah because she sincerely bowed before Him, asking Him to give her one son and promising she would give this child back to Him if He blessed her in this way. God heard her cry: she got pregnant. Then when Samuel was weaned, sure enough, she gave him back to God. For this act of faithfulness, God blessed her with three more sons and two daughters.

God's blessings are numberless. As He did with Hannah, if you are faithful to Him, He will give you more blessings than you ever thought possible. Sure, He blesses us anyway, but the rewards are even greater when we are faithful to Him.

I thank God for delivering me from my unfaithfulness to Him. You may not know when God will work things out, and it may look hopeless from where you stand, but He is Omniscient! He doesn't require that you worry about how He is going to do what you asked Him to do. Trust Him. Only trust Him. God will make a way out of no way. Look at what He did for Hannah. There was no technology back then to help a barren woman bear children. God's divine power alone created that miracle.

Know His power today. Praise the Lord, for there is none above Him!

Love,

Kelli Raí

Shower Him with Love

Psalm 116:1, 2 (NLT) *"I love the Lord because he hears my voice and my prayers for mercy. Because he bends down to listen, I will pray as long as I have breath!"*

Hello Beautifuls,

I was inspired last night in rehearsal to tell the Lord just how much I love Him. So many times when we pray, we ask for things without going down the line of reasons why we love God so much. We go to God like a Santa in the sky and ask for help, material goods, money, etc. But, that is not the kind of relationship He wants to have with us. God wants us to accept His love and the good things He has in store for us. He also loves it when we give Him praise and tell Him how much we love Him. He's so good to us, providing our every need; protecting us from danger; listening to everything we have to say; watching over us; dwelling with us when we invite Him into our presence; blessing us; He smiling upon us... the list goes on and on.

David created love songs and love poems to God. We can look at Psalms for an example of how to bathe God in the love we have for Him. You know, I shouldn't even be alive right now. The fact that I am breathing, have been blessed with a wonderful husband and am raising three beautiful children, should prompt me to shower God with my love in every breath I take.

I'm writing this today to encourage you. Tell God how much you love Him: write Him a song or poem, write a list of reasons why you love Him so much, meditate, tell someone else about Him. If it nourishes us to hear from our loved ones that they love us, don't you think God wants to hear it from us?

"**I love the Lord** because he hears my voice and my prayers for mercy. **Because he bends down to listen**, I will pray as long as I have breath!"

Love,

Kelli Raí

Breakthrough

Psalm 37:5 (KJV) "Commit thy way unto the Lord; trust also in Him; and He shall bring it to pass."

Hello Beautifuls,

I must testify about God's goodness and faithfulness. For the past few months, I have been very defiant towards God and basically living outside of His will for my life. I would say no to His prodding to allow Him to restore me. Recently, however, I could ignore Him no longer and gave my Self and my will over to Him **completely**.

When He started breaking me down, I felt like I had gotten body-slammed! It hurt a lot, but God comforted me the entire time; so much so, I asked Him to keep breaking me until He can take me where I need to be and mold me into the woman He would have me be. Now, I've always been taught that certain things come through fasting and praying. Well, I needed answers and guidance, so I decided to fast a couple days. He broke the chains that bound me to my sins! And it didn't take months or years to do! The Lord revealed Himself and His guidance in so many ways. He gave clear answers so that I didn't need to question. He also gave me discernment because I asked Him for it.

There are some things being worked through in my life that normally would frazzle me and have me on edge. I have such **peace**! I wouldn't trade this peace for anything in the world. I'm still fasting and praying and reading His word, looking to Him to lead and take control.

Be encouraged today that when you honestly submit your will to God and trust that He will take care of you, give you answers, be with you, give you a breakthrough, etc. Life is too short to be caught up in craziness. God can deliver you, and He wants to be your Focus, your Guide, your Help, and your Savior. Let Him. Let go of what's keeping you from Him.

Love,

Kelli Raí

I am Healed!

John 5:6-9 (NLT) "When Jesus saw him and knew he had been ill for a long time, he asked him, 'Would you like to get well?' 'I can't, sir,' the sick man said, 'for I have no one to put me into the pool when the water bubbles up. Someone else always gets there ahead of me.' Jesus told him, 'Stand up, pick up your mat, and walk!' Instantly, the man was healed! He rolled up his sleeping mat and began walking! But this miracle happened on the Sabbath."

Hello Beautifuls,

The beginning of 2007, God set me up for healing. The week prior to the healing, I fasted for seven days. I wasn't as diligent as I should have been in seeking the Lord, so He sought me out. The Thursday before the healing day was filled with my showering God with love, and this continued through Friday. On Friday night, God spoke to me about the healing I'd been asking for—an issue that has plagued me for some time.

Some time before, I made a covenant with God that when I finished a particular book that dealt with one of my issues, He would bless me with the ability to do another concert. (I was telling God what to do.) I believed I would be healed after I finished the book. Well I hadn't finished the book because of various excuses, and I was not able to do a concert. I wasn't healed. These thoughts ran through my head as I went to sleep, after I had thanked God for keeping His promises (because He always does, even when we don't keep ours). We should praise God for His promises, even when they've not yet been fulfilled, for He is a promise keeper.

The sermon on the following Sabbath was about effective ministry. The subject spoke loudly to me. The pastor referenced John 5:1-11, the story of Jesus healing the lame man at the pool of Bethesda. When the pastor was expounding on Jesus' asking the man if he wanted to be healed, God spoke directly to me. He said, "Kelli, do you want to be healed?" I was dumbfounded. I actually looked around because His voice was so clear to me. "Huh?" I exclaimed in my mind. "Yes!" I pictured me throwing out the book because the book itself did not contain my healing; Jesus is the One who heals! "You are healed. Tell everybody." I immediately thanked Him and was almost too overwhelmed to sing with the praise team at the end of the service.

We need to make sure that covenants with God are from Him. If we do things our way, we will limit ourselves. I had to be reminded that healing comes from Him, not from anything I could say or do. But God said I would be healed in the spring and He healed me before it even started.

Stay faithful and follow Him. Let Him guide you. God is still in the healing business. He still works miracles. I am a witness! He healed me!

Love,

Kelli Raí

No Issue Too Small

Psalm 8: 4-5 (NKJV) "What is man that You are mindful of him, And the son of man that You visit him? For You have made him a little lower than the angels, And You have crowned him with glory and honor"

Hello Beautifuls,

I have been asked why I look to God for guidance in my life. This person questioning me pretty much said that I'm blessed and God isn't going to be worried about my little issues. I had to let this person know that God *is* concerned with me because I'm His baby and He cares about me. And my issues aren't little to me!

David pointed out that God is mindful of us and He communes with us. The verse James 4:8 says, "Draw near to God and He will draw near to you." Don't let anyone tell you that God is not concerned with the matters in your life. God created us to commune and dwell with Him. He is omnipresent (everywhere at once) and He is omniscient (knows all). He loves each of us, and wants us to live with Him in Heaven when Jesus returns to take us home. He sent Jesus to die for us so we can accept the plan of salvation and can be saved, in spite of our sinful nature.

So, I say to you today, don't try to just deal with your problems on your own. Let God have control of your life. He will bring order to your chaos; I'm a witness! You will FAIL every time when you try to do it on your own. Only in Him can you find true solution, true conversion, true willpower, true healing, and true recovery from addiction. He cares about what's going on in your life. Let Him help you. Don't make Him your co-pilot, you be the co-pilot, let Him be the PILOT!

Stay strong and be encouraged today.

Love,

Kelli Raí

Letting Go

Romans 8:12 (NLT) "Therefore, dear brothers and sisters, you have no obligation to do what your sinful nature urges you to do."

Hello Beautifuls,

I had a great conversation with my close friend whom I call my "Jelly" sister. She is being purged of some things that are hindering her growth in God. Jelly was telling me about the emotional pain she was in, letting go of these earthly things that she so loves. I listened and conversed with her for about 2 hours. I thank God that she called me because it inspired me to do some soul searching of my own.

The wonderful thing about Jesus is that He died for our sins and not only that; He helps us when we are ready to turn our backs on sin. Yes, it is a painful process, but we must go through the fire to come out pure gold. The pain will not last eternally and we will be better for it when we overcome. The passage I urge you to read today is Romans 8:1-15.

It's encouraging to look back on what Jesus has done, and continues to do for us. What stands out for me are verses 12-15 which state: "So, dear brothers and sisters, you have no obligation whatsoever to do what your sinful nature urges you to do. For if you keep on following it, you will perish. But if *through the power of the Holy Spirit* you turn from it and its evil deeds, you will live. For all who are led by the Spirit of God are children of God. So, you should not be like cowering, fearful slaves. You should behave instead like God's very own children, adopted into His family--calling him 'Father, dear Father.'"

Through the strength and encouragement of the Holy Spirit, we don't have to be slaves to sin because we are children of God. He is our Daddy. He protects and saves us. We have to do our part and stay in relationship with Him so that He can connect with us. Only He can save us from the powers of Satan. It's a painful process when we are purged from the sins that we love and have nurtured. That's something no one talks about: the fact that coming out of sin is painful. However, in the end, we will be so relieved and freed from those chains! Through the process, Jesus is ever present. We will not go through it alone.

If there is anything you need to overcome, He's waiting for you to ask Him to take it and He's there to take you by the hand and lead you to victory. Praise God for His love for and constant care of us. Take comfort in His word today.

Love,

Kelli Raí

I am Looking Out for You

Jeremiah 29:11-13 (KJV) "For I know the thoughts that I think toward you, saith the LORD, thoughts of peace, not of evil, to give you an expected end. Then ye shall call upon me, and ye shall go and pray unto me, and I will hearken unto you. And ye shall seek me, and find me, when ye shall search for me with all your heart."

Hello Beautifuls,

"I got your back even when you don't think I do," the Lord said to me early one morning. I hadn't been talking with God like I should have when He sent me that message. Later that morning, I was looking for a parking space and I found one but I didn't listen when the Spirit said, "Park in that space across the street." I went ahead and parked at another meter but when I passed the meter where I should have parked, the space was available and there was 44 minutes paid on the meter. That's when God told me that He still has my back. See, I had an ongoing prayer pact at that time with God that when I got to work, He would help me find a free space or a 12-hour meter. I tell you He blessed me with parking, which may seem trivial to some but it was a big deal for me. This particular morning, I wasn't tuned in to Him, so I didn't receive the full blessing He had for me concerning parking.

Here's the lesson: if I'm not tuned into Him via worship, prayer, reading the Word, keeping my mind on Him, I feel separated from Him. The feeling of separation causes me to think that I'm not loved and that He's not looking out for me. In reality, He is still looking out for me. Hebrews 13:5 says "... for God has said, 'I will never fail you. I will never abandon you.'" From that we learn that He watches over us. His mind is ever toward us. I will remember that the next time I'm too tired to get on my knees to pray or too distracted to read His Word. I will remember that the next time my car is still running even though I'm a month overdue getting an oil change. I will remember that the next time there is a kitchen full of food but we still can afford to go out to eat. I will remember that when I allow the television to put me to bed and I only say a quick thank You when I wake up in the morning.

His mind is ever towards me. My mind should ever be towards Him. No one loves me and cares for me like He does. God's love can never be replaced with frivolity of this earth. Man's love can't match the strength and wonder of His love. So, today, reflect on the love of God and how it positively affects your life. Ask Him to shine through you today.

Love,

Kelli Raí

Fasting

Mark 9:29 (KJV) "And he said unto them, this kind can come forth by nothing, but by prayer and fasting."

Hello Beautifuls,

Very often when I hear people talk about faith, I've heard the phrase, "I have faith that God can move a mountain if it needs to be moved." When I hear the phrase, I always ask in myself, "You really think that God would move a mountain? Would it really be necessary?" I know that the statement is rhetorical but we really should search ourselves to see how strong our faith is. What are you willing to do to prove your faith in God?

In a Sabbath school lesson, there was a passage from Mark 9:14-29 about a boy who was possessed with a demon that made him foam at the mouth and grind his teeth together. It threw the boy on the ground and into fires and water to kill him. The parents brought the boy to the disciples to cast out the demon but they could not. The disciples argued amongst themselves, and then brought the matter to Jesus. The father of the child asked Jesus to do what He could. Jesus told the father that if he believes, all things are possible [in other words, have faith that the demon can be cast out]. The father of the boy cried out that he believed and for Jesus to help him in his lack of faith. Jesus cast out the demon. When the disciples asked why they couldn't do it, Jesus told them that some things only come of fasting and praying.

Fasting strengthens your faith. Fasting is omitting one or many things from your diet. When you have a pang of desire for the thing or things you have omitted, it's a reminder of why you are fasting, and then you pray. This binds you to the Lord causing you to interact with Him more than usual. In turn, He connects with you. He gives answers. He gives deliverance. Every time I fast, I have a breakthrough at the end. It can happen for you too. If you are earnestly seeking God, you will find Him. If you are earnestly seeking His truth, you will be blessed with it. There are some issues, diseases, and sins that can only be overcome by fasting and praying. Don't be afraid to seek God through fasting. He wants us to try Him then prove Him.

I pray that your faith in the Lord be strengthened.

Love,

Kelli Raí

Gossip

Proverbs 12:22 (NLT) ***"The Lord detests lying lips, but he delights in those who tell the truth."***

Hello Beautifuls,

I've been impressed to talk about gossip today. Years ago, I was watching Good Morning America and there was a segment on four women who got fired for gossiping at work about a relationship between the town administrator and another employee. Now, to some, this may seem an extreme punishment. Their "pink slips" stated that they were fired for engaging in "Gossip, whispering, and [creating] an unfriendly environment, causing poor morale and interfering with the efficient performance of town business." The gossipers' argument was that they were on their lunch break and the conversation was more or less along the lines of: "Did you hear that? So did I!" But the story was not true.

Most of social media, news and radio are built on gossiping about famous people. That's why paparazzi are employed; scavengers who make it impossible for the famous to live private lives. If you've ever been talked about and found out about it, you know the pain of it. Sometimes, people can carelessly make up stories and spread untruths about people. Or, they can take a little truth and run with it until it becomes a horrible lie that everyone is gossiping about. Either way it can become very destructive in many ways. If it happens at work, it makes you want to quit. If it happens at school, it makes you want to drop out. In the church, it makes you feel alienated and you could lose your faith. It can bring on depression and anxiety.

The Lord doesn't like for us to lie. As a matter of fact, He dislikes lying so much, the ninth Commandment states: "thou shalt not bare false witness against thy neighbour." Translation: don't lie on anybody. If you hear something about someone and you don't know if it's true or false, keep it to yourself. If you hear a story and you know it's true, keep it to yourself. If you tell anyone, tell God. What good will it do to tell someone's business? It does much good to just relay it to God in prayer to help improve the person's situation. In that you will also be blessed.

Love,

Kelli Raí

Who has Your Heart?

Isaiah 53:3 (NLT) "He was despised and rejected--a man of sorrows, acquainted with the bitterest grief. We turned our backs on him and looked the other way when he went by. He was despised and we did not care."

Hello Beautifuls,

Recently, I've been doing some soul searching. I once heard a sermon in which the speaker talked about how if God does not have our hearts, when we praise Him He can't bear to hear our praise (Isaiah 1:11-15). When I heard those words, I decided to do some soul searching. I asked myself, does God have my heart? Or am I just going through the motions with Him? And in this day and time, can I afford to keep my heart from Him? Can I really say that I love Jesus in the true meaning of the word love?

As humans, we have a pull to sin. We can't turn away from it with our own strength. When we revel in sin, we do exactly what the verse above, Isaiah 53:3, says. We turn our backs on Jesus without caring about Him and all that He did to save us. What must happen is for us to make a conscious decision to be willing to leave our sins (especially the favorites) behind and submit ourselves to Him. We must make daily time for Him in a quiet place where we can talk to Him and where we will hear when He speaks to us. We have to recognize that He is ever present and that we need for Him to deliver us from sin every day.

When we are pained by the temptation that we will inevitably face, we must learn to run the other way and ask God to strengthen us. We are strengthened in God through worship, through His word, through His love, and through His power. It's worth finding out the wonderful things that will happen in our lives and the wonders God will do through us when we decide to really give our hearts to Him. The blessing is that He is there waiting with His hand stretched out to lead us to victory.

Praise God!

Love,

Kelli Raí

Don't Pray and Worry

Psalm 22:1-2 (NLT) "My God, my God, why have you abandoned me? Why are you so far away when I groan for help? Every day I call to you, my God, but you do not answer. Every night you hear my voice, but I find no relief."

Hello Beautifuls,

Have you ever gone through something where you asked the Lord to guide you and/or take care of something for you and it seems like He didn't respond? Sometimes, when that happens, you're prompted to start worrying and stressing over the issue. That happened to David. But soon after David cried out to God, he quickly followed up with (verses 3-5) "Yet you are holy, enthroned on the praises of Israel. Our ancestors trusted in you, and you rescued them. They cried out to you and were saved. They trusted in you and were never disgraced."

If you're going to trust God with your problems or issues and place them in His hands, you have to leave them with Him. Remind yourself that He has always come through for you. Remind yourself that He even goes all out for you! That's why you must give Him praise no matter what your circumstance looks like. You can cry to God because He's your Father. He can receive it. But after that, you have to follow up with praises and some memories of when He went to bat for you and succeeded!

When you give something to God, He hears you and He takes on the responsibility. He's not going to give you a play by play of the plan. You have to have faith, hold on, and wait for it to play out. Meanwhile, give Him the praise and remind yourself of your past of when God had your back.

Love,

Kelli Raí

When Death Comes

Isaiah 40:9b (NLT) "... Tell the towns of Judah, 'Your God is coming!'"
Isaiah 65:17, 20a (NLT) "Look! I am creating new Heavens and a new earth, and no one will even think about the old ones anymore. No longer will babies die when only a few days old. No longer will adults die before they have lived a full life...."

Hello Beautifuls,

When death happens suddenly and my heart is heavy I have to remind myself of something happy. I need a hopeful thing to hold on to. I try to remember to be happy that God is coming soon. I praise Him for the fact that He will one day soon wipe the tears from all of our eyes and rescue us from this life when He returns again in the clouds of glory. We will all be changed in a moment, in the twinkling of an eye (1Corinthians 15:52). I praise Him for constantly comforting us and providing for us! I praise Him that I can wake up in the morning with a smile on my face. Let everything that has breath praise the Lord!

When my cousin, Michael Parker, passed away quickly and suddenly, it seemed as though a bright light had gone out. He was only 35. He was always positive, happy, loving, and caring. Michael was a person who was actually jolly most of the time! This was a big blow to all who loved him. But I took comfort in knowing that I will see him when Jesus comes again. We'll all rejoice in Zion together. That's what I'm looking forward to. I miss him greatly. There are many of us who are mourning the loss of Michael, but we will definitely see him again at that appointed time, which is definitely coming soon.

Remember to tell your loved ones how much you love and appreciate them. Life is short: even if you live until you're 97, it's short. Take the time to enrich someone else: doing so makes the heavy load a little lighter.

Love,

Kelli Raí

Praise God!

Philippians 4:6, 7 (NLT) "Don't worry about anything, instead pray about everything. Tell God what you need, and thank him for all he has done. Then you will experience God's peace, which exceeds anything we can understand. His peace will guard your hearts and minds as you live in Christ Jesus."

Hello Beautifuls,

God is SO GOOD! I can't help but give Him praise in my day-to-day conversations. He has blessed me immeasurably. He's blessed my family immeasurably. He is doing so many great things in the lives of my friends and acquaintances! Praise God for His goodness and His mighty acts! Praise God for His consistent, unfailing love and His mercy! Praise God for life and salvation and peace!

Even in sadness, I've learned to give God praise. Praising is something that you may have to teach yourself to do, especially if it wasn't a part of your upbringing. Maybe it was a part of your upbringing but you were uncomfortable with it. Praise pleases God and in turn He gives you peace in your circumstances. If you haven't done it, try it. If you are feeling down, push yourself to think of the good things He's done for you. Think about how much He cares for you. Sing a song of His goodness. Open up your Bible and read something in the book of Psalms, which is full of His praises. You will experience His unexplainable peace.

I really love God. I just wanted to share that with all of you. I hope that your days are bright and full of loveliness.

Love,

Kelli Raí

Keep Pushing

Philippians 3:13, 14 (NLT) "No, dear brothers and sisters, I have not achieved it, but I focus on this one thing: Forgetting the past and looking forward to what lies ahead, I press to reach the end of the race and receive the heavenly prize for which God, through Jesus Christ, is calling us."

Hello Beautifuls,

Have you ever been faced with something major that made you just want to give up and do something different, or just do nothing at all? It could be something like returning to school to finish a degree, or broaching a subject with a loved one that may cause them to blow up at you, or giving up on a diet because it's too hard to change the way you eat. My first instinct is always to give up but I've learned over time that giving up is the same as failing a test. You could really miss out on a great opportunity if you run away from a challenge.

One day I was toying with cancelling my physical therapy appointment because one of the various excuses I was willing to use (there were many). I was thinking of quitting the physical therapy course altogether because, was it really helping me with my pain? (I had only been twice, by the way.) However, I went to my appointment anyway. I'm so glad that I did! The air in the physical therapy office seemed weird. There weren't as many patients in there as usual and there were new people behind the desk. The therapists seemed a bit uptight. The therapist that worked me out at my last appointment approached me as I was filling out patient forms again. She informed me that they just went through a change in company and everything was in disarray. She went on to tell me about how some of her co-workers were upset and she herself was ready to strangle somebody! I finished filling out paper work and we started my therapy course. I kept it light, kept smiling, made jokes and tried to make sure she and possibly others laughed. I was determined to be a light in her dark day. She and her co-workers may have felt like giving up. I wanted them to have reason to keep pushing on.

Do you feel like giving up? Don't give up! Keep pushing. Maybe you can be a help to someone else as a result of pushing through. Maybe you can prove to yourself that you can actually accomplish whatever it is that seems to hard. Maybe the prayers that you pray for the person you want to give up on are the very prayers that will transform their life. So, don't give up. Please, don't give up.

Love,

Kelli Raí

Henry

Psalm 32:8 (NLT) The Lord says, "I will guide you along the best pathway for your life. I will advise you and watch over you."

Hello Beautifuls,

God is still in the business of working miracles. Something odd happened after church last week. When I got out of my car to go into my house I noticed a man that I'd never seen before, walking up my street. He got my attention and asked if I knew where a certain church was. I didn't understand his question so he walked across the street to me and repeated himself. I told him to come to my doorstep and I'd look it up for him. I went into my house for a second trying to figure out how to look up this church. (I know that there's a church near my house but I have no idea how to get there.) He told me that the postman told him to walk the short path through some trees and he'd see a church. He ended up on my street instead. His name was Henry.

Henry seemed exasperated and as I tried to look up the church on my phone, he told me about all he'd been through that day. He leveled with me that he was trying to collect enough money to catch the bus to Durham where he was from. This man had a Spanish accent and I could see that he was Latino. Henry quickly pulled out his passport, which had his Social Security card in it to prove to me that he was an American citizen (which by the way didn't make a difference to me: he was still a stranger). He told me that he had walked all day and hadn't eaten. I ran back inside and got him a sleeve of crackers, an apple, water and a chair, then rejoined him on my porch.

Henry seemed to be near tears as he told me about how the entire day he'd been treated horribly by people. At a church, he was told to leave by a deacon or elder. Henry asked him, "Why should I leave? God doesn't see our skin color, he sees us inside! We're not that different." When he approached an older woman of color, she looked down on him and told him God wouldn't help him until he changed his "lifestyle." He responded, "Lifestyle? You don't know anything about me!" After that he was kicked out. He then went to McDonald's to ask for a bit of food, he was told he needed to lose weight—he didn't need any food. The police at McDonald's attempted to take him to a psych ward but he stood his ground and ended up having to show his passport. He then walked into an eatery where the waitress had no money to give him but she prayed with him that God would help him find his way home. Then, he went to the Catholic church; which was closed. He sat on the steps and cried big tears. When he started walking again, he ran into a postman that guided him to another church but he ended up meeting me instead.

I invited Henry in and he said he'd stay on the step, at first, but I convinced him that it was ok. He came in and sat down. I made him a sandwich and some tea (and prepared another sandwich and cupcakes for him to take on his trip). Meanwhile, he went over the story again... and deeper into his story. He was not used to asking for things. He'd worked for Marriott for 16 years, became a naturalized citizen during that time. Marriott had recently fired him. His mother had died recently. Henry was so depressed. He was just trying to get home. He loves God. His faith was renewed with the help we were giving him.

My mother and I put some money together which turned out to be the exact amount of money Henry needed for the bus. Henry almost didn't want to accept the money but we wouldn't take no for an answer. When my husband got home from church, I had him drive Henry to Union Station to catch his bus. Before he left Henry remarked, "I almost felt at home." (I wondered, myself, while Henry sat with us, if we'd been in the presence of an angel in disguise.)

Henry coming into our home reminded me of how much God loves us and takes care of us. In Henry's words, "The postman told me I'd find a church through the woods and I found my temple on the hill." The way he persevered through his difficulty all the while believing that God would help him somehow, and then God delivering him to people who would take care of him lets me know that God is real. God still works miracles. He's still guiding us. He is interested in delivering us and even revealing himself to us in different ways.

I challenge you to believe that God is bigger than any problem you could ever face. Believe that God will help you. There is NOTHING too hard for my God to work out!

Love,

Kelli Raí

He's Our Everything

2 Corinthians 9:10 (NLT) "For God is the one who provides seed for the farmer and then bread to eat. In the same way, he will provide and increase your resources and then produce a great harvest of generosity in you."

Hello Beautifuls,

Don't we serve a marvelous God? He is the provider of all our needs: money, food, clothing, and a roof over our heads. The list goes on and on. I just wanted to praise God for reminding me today that He is my Provider so I won't allow myself to worry when things look bleak. I have to remember that He hasn't failed me yet.

When I had my first two children out of wedlock, He provided for me both times. With my first child, I got to stay home for 6 months and God provided. With my second child, God provided so that I stayed at home for a year. Both times, I didn't have a job and God kept those who took care of us; therefore, God kept us. Now I'm married, we have three children, and they're all in private school. God has provided so that neither my husband nor I would have to get a second job to keep up payments. More than that, God has sustained us, not just at those times that I mentioned but constantly.

If you're facing some financial issues, pray and ask God to give you the opportunity for you to be generous, even if you haven't been a good steward with what He has provided in the past. Remind Him that His word says that He's the one "who provides the seed for the farmer and then bread to eat." Ask Him to provide for you so that you and your family will not be in want. And when your breakthrough comes - and it will come - be generous with what He gives you.

Don't fret; He's not failed yet. He can do anything but fail. Hold fast to His promises. Fast and pray. Let Him guide you in reading His Word. And don't forget to give Him praise. You can't be sad if you're praising Him. Praise brings forth joy and gladness.

Love,

Kelli Raí

Praise While You Wait

Psalm 27:13, 14 (NIV) I am still confident of this: I will see the goodness of the LORD in the land of the living. Wait for the LORD; be strong and take heart and wait for the LORD.

Hello Beautifuls,

You know, it seems that if it's not one thing, it's another. I encountered some disappointment these last three days. The first day, the Holy Spirit reminded me that I should praise Him even through my disappointment. I really didn't feel like it, but I turned on some praise music and before I knew it I was singing and clapping praises to God. I felt no sadness at all. The second day I felt down again, but I put on some praise music and was, again, rejuvenated. Today is the third day, and I feel fine.

The thing I'm waiting for hasn't come through yet, but God has already taken care of my family and me. I don't have to worry about anything, ever. He put a song on my heart this morning "Have Thine own way Lord, have Thine own way... while I am waiting, yielded and still." Right now, I have to wait on the Lord and wait patiently. I must be faithful. He's never let me down, so there's no reason why I should be impatient; He's going to come through for me. I must allow Him to work things His way since I gave Him my burden.

His way is always best.

Love,

Kelli Raí

Hope for the Hopeless

Lamentations 3:21, 22 (NLT) "Yet I still dare to hope when I remember this: The faithful love of the Lord never ends! His mercies never cease."

Hello Beautifuls,

Lately, I've been stressed out about money. The financial crisis has been sitting on top of my bank accounts for some time now for various reasons. I've cried about it; prayed about it; tried to keep my chin up about it; but still I feel plagued and worried. In the back of my mind, the word "faithful" keeps chiming. Then I say, "Lord, I've tried to be faithful with my tithe and offering!" He replies, "Then you'll be okay." But I continue to complain.

Since I decided to complain to God, He led me to Lamentations 3. It's pretty much nothing but complaining until verse 21: "Yet, I still dare to hope when I remember this: (v22) The faithful love of the Lord never ends! [Hebrew reads: The faithful love of the Lord keeps us from destruction.] His mercies never cease. (v23) Great is his faithfulness; his mercies begin afresh each morning." I will not be destroyed by my circumstances! With every morning I receive mercy!

Thank God! He is there to guide me in my sadness. He turns hopelessness into great hope! He has increased my faith in Him by reminding me that He's never failed me. I've been here before and He delivered me then; He will deliver me again! So today, seek God's guidance.   Ask Him to remind you of His faithfulness so that our faith can increase.   Perhaps His faithfulness to you can encourage someone else who may be facing hard times. Be faithful!

Love,

Kelli Raí

He Fights Our Battles

Exodus 14:14 (NLT) "The Lord Himself will fight for you. Just stay calm."

Hello Beautifuls,

Isn't God great? I'm so glad that we serve a God Who will engage in battle for us. This week I prayed and thanked God for being my warrior, and then my father introduced the above verse to me not knowing what I had prayed. God is our warrior. He confirmed it in His word to me when I was unsure.

Many of us are battling things in our lives that we have a hard time fighting. We have a hard time giving it to God to fight because we want to do things our way and have control over the matter. The longer we try to take control of situations, the longer it takes for the situation to get solved. Now, it is true that we have to make the decision to stop smoking, to stop being promiscuous, to stop drinking, to stop abusing drugs, to love ourselves, to stop overeating, to walk away from a toxic relationship, etc. It takes a degree of restraint to stop certain behaviors, but God will be in front of you fighting the battle so that you can have victory over the sin/situation/behavior.

God's way sometimes seems off and out of the way. When He led the Israelites out of Egypt, He didn't take the short route, He took them through the wilderness by the Red Sea. He blocked the Egyptians from seeing them when they were in hot pursuit of the Israelites. Then He parted the Red Sea and the Israelites crossed on DRY GROUND. Then God drowned the entire Egyptian army. God fought their battle. When it seemed like certain doom, God, who knows and sees all, saved the day! Not only that, later on, He sprinkled food from Heaven when they were in the midst of the wilderness and had run out of food! He provides all your needs from fighting for you to feeding you. He's the ultimate security guard.

Allow God to fight all your battles. Make the decision to stop holding on to whatever it is that's causing you worry and stress and keeping you from God. Even if it seems like the path He's taking you on is out of the way, trust that He's protecting you. He'll give you strength to resist and He'll remind you to give your burdens and cares to Him. "The Lord Himself will fight for you. Just stay calm."

Love,

Kelli Raí

Unworthy

Psalm 92:1-2 (NIV) "It is good to praise the LORD and make music to your name, O Most High, to proclaim your love in the morning and your faithfulness at night."

Hello Beautifuls!

This message comes as a poem/prayer I wrote. Our God deserves love poems. David used to write Him love poems and love songs all the time. This one flowed from me this morning. I hope you enjoy it.

unworthy

i'm loving You
it's refreshing relieving to my soul
this love
i could never contain it all myself
makes me want to give You all of me and whatever is yet to come
You make me smile all over
i don't want to leave Your side
You laugh tenderness in the darkness of night
my name is always safe in Your mouth
when You speak my name
you speak positive truths into reality
i'm secure in knowing that You are loyal and steadfast
help me
help me love You like that
though I'm unworthy to ask of such an honor
help me
for Your love is the most beautiful ism i've ever experienced.

-Kelli Raí Collins

He'll Help Your Unbelief

Mark 9:24 (NIV) Immediately the boy's father exclaimed, "I do believe; help me overcome my unbelief!"

Hello Beautifuls,

I've found that one of the major things that keeps us from walking away from things that hold us back (sin) is the unbelief that we can let go; unbelief that God can really help us change our ways and bad habits. Do you know that He will help your unbelief? You have to pray and ask Him to help you believe that you can live a healthy life, that you can walk away from your destructive nature, and that you can surrender to Him.

I bought Tye Tribbett & GA's cd entitled "Life," when it came out and there are two songs that really ministered to me. One I'll mention today is about how there is an answer for you in God because He cares about you and loves you: you're never alone with His love, you don't have to cry or hide or hurt with His love. The line that spoke to me was "God loves you, you have a reason to live now... He loves you, now you can throw all those pills out." Those words spoke loud to me because I used to suffer extensively with depression. My lowest point was in college when, one day, I was going to buy sleeping pills, take the whole bottle, then just sleep... forever. Something told me to call my therapist first and she made me promise not to leave. I didn't go through with buying the sleeping pills and I haven't been low like that since. God helped me realize that I could live without being depressed. I still get sad sometimes, of course, but not depressed because God's strength saves me. I walked away from a depressed life and am better for it today! (Therapy was an important part of my healing.)

I want you to know that you, too, can walk into living a good and healthy life. You can be healed. If you don't believe, pray and ask God to help your unbelief. The story that I took the verse from was about a man's son who was possessed. He brought his son to Jesus to be healed. Jesus told him that the boy could be healed if he believed. And then he said, "I believe, help my unbelief." Jesus healed him. The boy was healed because his father asked for Jesus to help him with his shortcoming.

You can be healed. Your life can change for the better. Believe and ask; He will help you.

Love,

Kelli Raí

He's a Healer

Isaiah 26:3-4 (NLT) "You will keep in perfect peace all who trust in you, all whose thoughts are fixed on you! Trust in the Lord always, for the Lord God is the eternal Rock."

Hello Beautifuls,

Earlier this year, God healed me from Seasonal Affective Disorder. It's a condition I have suffered for years in the autumn months. Anyhow, I put God to the test this October. I truly have not suffered as I usually do. Usually I have a dead feeling in the pit of my stomach. I loathe having to go outdoors, even when it's sunny. My skin would crawl at the thought of air hitting my skin. I carried sadness with me at all times. All those issues, God wiped away with my acceptance of His healing. PRAISE GOD!!!

Just like "God don't like ugly", the devil don't like pretty. The devil is mad that I'm healed and not suffering in depression. I've been under direct attack of the enemy, but God has been my sword and shield. Though some things have saddened me, I have amazing strength from the Lord. Some days I think of the trials of that day or week and thank God that I made it through. Some mornings I'm amazed that the joy of the Lord really does meet me after crying and praying all night long. I have no desire to lie in bed all day and hide away from life. I don't carry my pain. I leave it with God and go on to do the things He has me to do. I thank God for healing me and delivering me and fighting for me.

I've shared all this to let you know that God still works miracles. A doctor can tell you one thing and God can still heal you completely. I'm a witness that He is a Healer, a Deliverer, a Doctor, a Lawyer, a Stronghold, a Provider, and a Father. If you haven't already, please accept Him in all His ways today. Let Him deliver you from the stronghold of sin.

Love,

Kelli Raí

Change is Possible

Malachi 3:3 (NLT) "He will sit like a refiner of silver, burning away the dross. He will purify the Levites, refining them like gold and silver so that they may once again offer acceptable sacrifices to the Lord."

Hello Beautifuls,

I had an experience Saturday evening that was such a major lesson from God; I had to share it today. There is a man from whom I try to keep my distance because I know of some of personal business (or sins) and it really turns me off. I pass judgment on him every time I see him. If I see him first, I do my best to stay out of his sight. We usually see each other at church or at gospel concerts. Saturday, after a concert at church, I couldn't avoid him. He actually encouraged me after the concert and God spoke to me as this man was conversing with me. God told me to be still, to be kind and to listen. He said, "I can use whomever I want to bless you. You are no better than he is. Sin is sin and you don't know where he is in his life right now. You thank him for encouraging you."

So there I was, smiling at this man, engaging in conversation with him, AND thanking him. This is the same man that I judged with wrath because I felt that his sins were so horrible. But what if he were a murderer? In God's eyes, murdering is the same as me lying. If God can change the life and the ways of a liar, can He not also change the life and ways of a murderer? Can't our God do all things? Who am I to judge? God changed the ways of Saul who murdered the early Christians. He became a major apostle for Christ when he was changed.

Just like God does with me, He is refining others who believe in Him and that are open to being shaped by Him. God burns away the sins of our past and makes us new in Him. If we are open to being changed, He will change our sinful ways. It takes work on our part but change is possible. So, I'm no different from the man God used to bless me on Saturday night. I don't know where he is in his Christian walk, but it's not for me to know or to judge him on his past. I'm glad to learn that lesson.

Thank you, God for these precious lessons.

Love,

Kelli Raí

God is Perfection

Psalm 18:30 (NLT) "As for God, his way is perfect: the word of the LORD is tried: he is a buckler to all those that trust in him."

Hello Beautifuls,

I'm going to be straight with all of you. I found it especially hard to write anything this week because God is teaching me some cold, hard lessons. Like medicine, it was just really hard to swallow. He told me to write about it but I just couldn't bring myself to do it. Yet, here I am, knowing I'm going to get grief if I skip writing this message another day. Today's message is especially personal.

Sometimes when you ask God for something, He says no or wait. He does not always say, "yes." Sometimes when you ask Him to do something for you He does it in His time, not yours. When you ask to be first, He'll probably say, "Well, this time you'll be fourth. You have to bide your time. You can't lead until you follow." These kinds of lessons are hurtful and hard to take, but not a waste of time. In time, they will make you wise if you apply the lesson correctly.

We need to realize and remember that His way is perfect. It's perfect, it's perfect, it's perfect! When you step back and watch how He orchestrates everything perfectly in His way, you can breathe a sigh of relief and be thankful that you had nothing to do with it. You simply put it in His hands and *try* to patiently wait. A God that can create a universe from void (great planets to tiny microorganisms that live) can certainly create order in your chaotic life.

Just like we do with our children, He sometimes has to say, "Wait, I have this under control. I already know what needs to happen." Be still and know that He is God. I tend to stress out and then I feel humbled when I see all that He's doing "behind the scenes." When you pray and put your matters into His hands, He doesn't ignore you. He really does love you and is taking care of you.

Love,

Kelli Raí

Discernment

Revelation 22:7, 12-13 (NLT) "Look, I am coming soon! Blessed are those who obey the words of prophecy written in this book." "Look, I am coming soon, bringing my reward with me to repay all people according to their deeds. I am the Alpha and the Omega, the First and the Last, the Beginning and the End."

Hello Beautifuls,

I have been bombarded with so much information in the last two days; I just want to run away from it all. It is very apparent that we're not fighting "against flesh and blood but against principalities, against powers, against the rulers of the darkness of this world, against spiritual wickedness in high places." (Eph. 6:12, KJV) Many things that we think are harmless like music, TV, and movies really have a lot of underlying spiritual themes. With the nearness of Christ's return, things are only going to get more intense. Satan is going all out to get us and keep us in his grasp, and he's really focusing on our children and youth. They are our future leaders.

I just want to encourage each of you to pray for discernment. We are to guard the avenues of our souls. We need to be aware and allow God to be our Security Guard of our souls. If you are listening to something and it goes against your core beliefs, turn it off. If something comes on TV and you don't feel right watching it, turn it off. I was watching a popular Halloween cartoon special last night and couldn't believe that I was uncomfortable with them dressing up as witches and ghosts and going trick-or-treating. I let my kids watch it and didn't turn it off though it wasn't sitting right with me. I've been watching Charlie Brown Halloween special since my childhood! But the tradition must end with me. I know better now. I can't support it.

You may not be convicted the same as I am on the same issues but that was just an example of not exposing yourself to something you're not comfortable experiencing. The more God blesses you with the spirit of discernment, the more you will be unsettled with things that go against your core beliefs. Don't settle for doing something just because it's tradition or because no one else has a problem with it. Dare to be a Daniel! Dare to stand alone; dare to have a purpose firm; dare to make it known!

Love,

Kelli Raí

A Little Can Mean So Much

1 Peter 4:11 (NLT) "Do you have the gift of speaking? Then speak as though God himself were speaking through you. Do you have the gift of helping others? Do it with all the strength and energy that God supplies. Then everything you do will bring glory to God through Jesus Christ. All glory and power to him forever and ever! Amen."

Hello Beautifuls,

I was delighted to find out, yesterday evening, that chivalry is not dead. Two people (count 'em, two!) offered their seats to me on the train. I thankfully declined, but I felt so good to have received the offering. God really blessed me at the end of an emotionally trying workday.

The simple act of someone's willingness to give up their seat for me made me think of what a blessing it is to help others and to receive help from others. When you're in need, aren't you thankful when someone assists you? When it's convenient, or inconvenient for that matter, doesn't it make you feel good to help someone that you're capable of helping? In the Bible, Peter says that helping others is a gift. I never thought of it that way. That means that when we help someone else, it's not only a blessing to the receiver but also a blessing to the helper. When we help others, we should do it with all the strength and energy that God supplies. God will give you STRENGTH and ENERGY when you are willing to use the gifts He's bestowed upon you.

This week, take time out to glorify God by using the gift of helping others. Not only will it make someone else feel good, it will make you feel good. Praise God for the gifts He's given!

Love,

Kelli Raí

Take a Stand

Revelation 3:15-16 (NLT) "I know all the things you do, that you are neither hot nor cold. I wish that you were one or the other! But since you are like lukewarm water, neither hot nor cold, I will spit you out of my mouth!"

Hello Beautifuls,

A couple weeks ago, I read about scientists displaying a fossilized hominid from which [they believe] humans evolved. According to scientists, it's 3 million years old. Friday night on Trinity Broadcasting Network, I saw a fictional "Christian" movie about these reporters trying to dissect the cause of UFO sightings. They were saying that UFOs and aliens were really demonic beings used to confuse people about the secret rapture that will happen during the seven years of tribulation in the last days. I was thinking, "What secret rapture and what seven years of tribulation?" I've read Revelation more than once and that was not a part of the last days described in the Bible. If I hadn't searched the scripture for myself and ask God for discernment, I surely would have been confused. It seemed to me that the devil was using a "Christian" movie to further put confusion in the minds of Christians, new believers, or people in search of truth.

We are experiencing the End of Days. We need to choose what we believe and where we stand with God. You need to pick a side and stand strong on it. This is not the time to try to be in the middle. God is turned off by the fact that we do not make a sound choice. Lukewarm isn't good enough. Joshua 24:15 says: "But if you refuse to serve the Lord, then choose today whom you will serve. Would you prefer the gods your ancestors served beyond the Euphrates? Or will it be the gods of the Amorites in whose land you now live? But as for me and my family, we will serve the Lord." You know the difference between right and wrong. So, where do you stand?

Love,

Kelli Raí

A Way Out

Exodus 14:13-14 (NLT) "But Moses told the people, 'Don't be afraid. Just stand still and watch the Lord rescue you today. The Egyptians you see today will never be seen again. The Lord himself will fight for you. Just stay calm.'"

Hello Beautifuls!

I was recently reminded of the story of when Moses led the children of Israel out of Egypt to the Promised Land. Soon after Pharaoh let them go, he and his army pursued them to kill them all. The Israelites were scared and angry when they realized they were caught between the Red Sea and the fast approaching Egyptian army. They saw no way out. Moses revealed to them that the very Egyptians who pursued them would be destroyed, and that God would fight for them. They wouldn't have to do a thing but trust Him.

It made me think that sometimes, in the midst of trying dilemmas or bad situations, we get down because we can only see the problem in hot pursuit coming up behind us and before us, a vast ocean of impossibilities. But, when presented with temptation, God always provides a way out. When we are in the midst of a storm, He always has an escape or haven for us to protect us from certain demise. We have to remember that He wants us to not only survive but to be successful in life. He doesn't guide us far in life only to abandon us in the midst of trouble.

Don't allow yourself to get sucked into despairing over issues. Don't allow yourself to get depressed because you keep making the same mistake over and over. Remember that God is here to help you. Rely on His strength everyday, every moment, and every second. Commit yourself to making good choices and keep your head up. You have the power (in Him) to truly overcome and be successful. Believe it!

Love,

Kelli Raí

Falling in Love with Jesus

John 15:4 (NLT) "Remain in me, and I will remain in you. No branch can bear fruit by itself; it must remain in the vine. Neither can you bear fruit unless you remain in me."

Hello Beautifuls,

I'm sorry I haven't sent a message since before the concert. Thank you for your prayers and for your presence at the concert. It was truly a blessing to me. My sisters flew out, my friend LaShawnda flew out, and my local family and friends showed up! Not to mention God showed up. It was definitely His concert. Mark Francis, one of my keyboardists, hadn't slept since Thursday because his wife, Alison, went into labor and had her baby on Saturday afternoon (the day of the concert). Nevertheless, she encouraged him to play for the concert anyway, and he did. The band was off the hook! The singers were fabulous! The concert was very successful. I can't wait to do another!

God sometimes speaks to me by putting a song on my heart. The song He put on my heart is "Falling in Love With Jesus" by Jonathon Butler and Kirk Whalum. It is a powerful song expressing the security and love one feels when you are "in love" with Jesus.

It made me question where my relationship with Jesus is: am I in love with Him or is He just some entity that I pray to who answers my prayers. Do I take the time to truly abide with Him so He can abide in me? Do I take enough time to study Him and learn Him making me love Him like I could love no other? Have I put limits on my love because I'm scared of experiencing a love that I could never explain through words?

John 15:4 states: "Remain in me, and I will remain in you. No branch can bear fruit by itself; it must remain in the vine. Neither can you bear fruit unless you remain in me." I guess that means that we should have constant communication with God. We have to humble ourselves and be vulnerable to His constant love and blessing. It would be different if we had to be vulnerable to a God that abuses us constantly but that's not the case. We have to be vulnerable to constant unconditional love and blessings and grace and mercy. That's a good thing.

The song says: "In His arms I feel protected, in His arms never disconnected, in His arms I feel protected. There's no place I'd rather be." I'd rather be walking around with God's peace and security inside than worry and doubt and sadness and loneliness. Those things always lurk in the shadows for me. So, I'm reminded that I have to take time to spend time in Him... remain in Him so that He can remain in me.

Ask Him today to show you how to love Him better.

Love,

Kelli Raí

You are Perfect?

Romans 12:2, 3 (NLT) "Don't copy the behavior and customs of this world, but let God transform you into a new person by changing the way you think. Then you will learn to know God's will for you, which is good and pleasing and perfect. Because of the privilege and authority God has given me, I give each of you this warning: Don't think you are better than you really are. Be honest in your evaluation of yourselves, measuring yourselves by the faith God has given us."

Hello, Beautifuls,

Have you ever felt like you were better than someone else? Be honest. Have you ever looked at someone else's flaws or shortcomings and convinced yourself that because you didn't have those particular problems that you were better than they are? I have. I've put myself a little (or a lot) higher than someone else because my sins weren't as extreme or as obvious as theirs. I've felt that I was better than someone else because his or her flaws were just weird, so I must be better.

This thought process is not of God. Yes, He calls us to perfection, but perfection is a lifelong journey. Being called to strive for perfection does not involve us comparing ourselves to others in any way. We should measure ourselves by the faith God has given us.

Humility is a part of the perfection process. In the Bible, God humbled great leaders and it was then (in their humble state) that they fulfilled their greatest purpose. Look at the lives of Joseph, Peter, Paul, and Samson. And I only mentioned four examples; there are many more. Humility is not puffed up. You can't be modest and arrogantly above someone else at the same time.

Today, let's be real with ourselves. Let's put forth effort to acknowledge that none of us is perfect and all of us are in need of God to help us get there. Let's be humble and put down our guard enough to help each other along this journey to Heaven.

Love,

Kelli Raí

We All Fall Down

Deuteronomy 31:8 (KJV) *"And the LORD, he it is that doth go before thee; he will be with thee, he will not fail thee, neither forsake thee: fear not, neither be dismayed."*

Hello Beautifuls,

Has it been one of those weeks for you? I've spoken to four people who are just ready for the week to be over. Admittedly, I am weary as I write this. However, I knew God had a message for me to give you, and everything came together this morning.

We are human and we fail. Even though we may overcome many things in our lives along our path to God, we fail God from time to time. In our failing, others around us who watch us (because we are being watched by others) may feel betrayed by our failure. When I use the word failure, I'm not using it to mean loser, I'm using it to mean falter.

A co-worker sent me an email of a press conference called by Bishop Weeks in his defense about him beating down his wife Juanita Bynum, a prominent speaker and gospel singer. I watched part of his statement. I then watched part of her statement. I was blown by the fact that her whole ministry is based on empowering yourself to keep from promiscuity and to leave abusive relationships and there she was in yet another abusive relationship. But I was passing judgment. I had to check myself.

Even though we may overcome sins that easily beset us we will still be tested. Satan also attacks our weakness. Knowing that, you need to continue to be consistent in your seeking God. Also, don't be quick to judge others. Because, though we may fail God, He never fails us. He had Moses tell the people in Deuteronomy 31: 6 and 8 "...he will not fail thee, nor forsake thee..." He told Joshua in Joshua 1:5 "... so I will be with thee: I will not fail thee, nor forsake thee." Jeremiah told us in Lamentations 3:22 that "...his compassions fail not." Overcoming sin is a lifelong journey. God is a constant and He will ever be with you and will never fail you nor forsake you, even if you happen to falter.

So, if you mess up, say to God, "I know you are with me and will never forsake me, please help me." When you hear news of someone faltering in his or her walk, say a prayer for him or her. That's the only way you will make it in this life. People will fail you. God never will.

Love,

Kelli Raí

Coming Soon

Luke 21:26-28 (NLT) "People will be terrified at what they see coming upon the earth, for the powers in the Heavens will be shaken. Then everyone will see the Son of Man coming on a cloud with power and great glory. So when all these things begin to happen, stand and look up, for your salvation is near!"

Hello Beautifuls,

I don't know about you, but more and more lately I'm hearing about the "End Times." For those of you not familiar with the phrase, it refers to this world coming to an end and Jesus coming to retrieve His people and take them to Heaven. Jesus spoke about this time of the end in the gospels (see Matthew 25 and Luke 21 for examples). At times, when you look at what could literally happen, and the chaos that could occur; you may feel scared, or maybe just uneasy. Fear is not the point of the End of Days. Jesus returning to take us home to heaven is the point.

In 2 Timothy 1:7 Paul writes, "For God has not given us a spirit of fear and timidity, but of power, love, and self-discipline." We should not be afraid of anything. If our economy crashes completely, all our rights are taken, and we have no jobs, we are still not to be afraid of our circumstances. Though the happenings may seem scary, if we have faith in God, we shouldn't have fear of anything. For hasn't God provided for us thus far? Hasn't He always taken care of us?

Look at the Israelites wandering in the desert for forty years. Didn't God provide them with manna from Heaven? I can look at my own life where things looked hopeless and God always came through for me. At the beginning of this month, we had negative dollars in the bank and a friend of ours, not knowing the situation, suggested we go shopping with him at a bulk grocery store. I said, "We can go on payday... the last day of this month." He said, "Let's worry about money later. Let's go now." We've had food overflowing in our freezer. Chicken for days! That's the kind of God I serve. He's the kind of God who doesn't put my business in the street and provides for my family and me in all kinds of methods.

Jesus is coming again soon. He will and has always provided for His people. The world is not going to get any better, no matter who we vote into office. The point is to grow closer to God. We should know Him better so that we'll recognize His voice when He guides us to do what He'll have us do. This is not a time to be scared or uneasy. The good thing is He's taking us home with Him! He's coming back again so that we can live forever!

Love,

Kelli Raí

Oh! How He Loves Us!

Psalm 89:1-2 (NLT) "I will sing of the Lord's unfailing love forever! Young and old will hear of your faithfulness. Your unfailing love will last forever. Your faithfulness is as enduring as the Heavens."

Hello Beautifuls,

This past week, I've been meditating on just how much God loves me [us]. The fact alone that Jesus limited Himself to become a human, lived a sinless life, then died on the cross so that we can one day live eternally with Him, floors me. He decided to meet us where we are, in flesh and blood, to relate to us and save us from eternal damnation. Now He lives on, in Heaven as 100% human and 100% God, dwelling in the Most Holy Place in the Heavenly sanctuary preparing to come and get us. Oh, what joy fills my heart at this knowing this!

This Sabbath was filled with praise for God. When I think of His goodness, I think back to how He protected me as I grew up. I think of how He blessed me with a discerning spirit so that I could hear and know His voice so that He can guide me. I remember being in danger, when my parents and sisters had no idea, and God delivered me to safety. I think of how He's given me a wonderful family. I remember waking up with wonderful love songs on my mind from Him to me and me back to Him. I know that He really, really, really loves me. He cares about the things that matter to me: small and great. I know that He really, really, really loves you too.

I have been so emotionally and spiritually full these past few days that I'm easily prone to tears. God had me talk and pray with a student who was having a difficult morning; it made a difference to us both. He had me share my love and admiration for a new friend. He had me share with my family that we need to give Him praise daily just because we love Him... and if *you* didn't know, praise will keep depression and sadness at bay. It will allow a place in your soul for His perfect peace. I'm so glad to have the opportunity to share God's love with you. He wants a relationship with you. If you seek Him, you will definitely find Him for He's right with you now. Though you may feel a separation, He's never left you. If you would just be open to Him, as scary as that may seem, He will take you places you'd never thought you'd go. You would receive such a blessing you wouldn't be able to keep it to yourself. This coming week, find time for praising and seeking the Lord. He wants you to.

Love,

Kelli Raí

The Original Plan

Revelation 3:20 (KJV) *"Behold, I stand at the door and knock: if any man hear my voice, and open the door, I will come in to him, and will sup with him, and he with me."*

Hello Beautifuls!

I had a character-building week. I learned two key lessons today: one had to do with double-checking; simply reading my own schedule that I wrote, and 112 unneeded cupcakes. The other lesson, the one I'll share with you now, has to do with communing with God.

I received a text message this week that talked about how we should carry around our Bibles the way we carry cell phones; how we should open the Bible and read it the way we utilize our phones and send/read text messages. I scanned it, deleted it, and moved on. I got the gist. No, I hadn't read the Bible, as I should have this week, outside of reading the Bible lesson to the class I've been substitute teaching. As the week went on, I realized that my cell phone is going to get cut off soon because I haven't paid last month's bill. I wanted to make sure all the family's necessities were met before I paid for any luxuries I may enjoy. I can't send text messages but I can receive calls right now - for maybe the next three days - then nothing, until I pay my bill. Even though my phone is like a security blanket for me (I take it wherever I go), I let my service get real shaky. It stressed me out for over an hour today!

It hit me when I got home that as attached as I am to my communication line with folks I like, I should be more attached to my communication with the Lord. I've prayed this week but they've been quick drive-by prayers. There's no excuse for not fully communing with the Lord. He is always present and accounted for; I'm the one who doesn't reach out to Him to complete the connection. I got off balance when I thought about not having my cell phone service to use. I should feel the same way about not being connected to God. He's the only One who truly keeps me balanced. It's laughable to think that my reliance on a phone would unbalance me!

What's the most important connection to have: new school technology or old school technology? God doesn't need a phone, car, plane, space shuttle, or computer to get with us. His original cordless plan was for us just to pray and He would hear us, listen, and speak back to us; which is still the plan and it's free with no hidden fees. The new technology will one day be obsolete.

The Lord is standing there knocking at our heart's door. He simply wants us to hear Him and answer so that He can share a meal with us, spend intimate time with us. He wants to feed us, if you will, and share in the process of getting fed. Will you answer?

Love,

Kelli Raí

Encourage Each Other

***Judges 20:22 (NLT)** "But the Israelites encouraged each other and took their positions again at the same place they had fought the previous day."*

Hello Beautifuls,

Does it ever feel to you that you are fighting a battle when you encounter difficulties in your home or at work? Sometimes you get thrown into battle when you least expect it. Other times, you can feel the battle coming on but you just don't know when the missiles are going to start flying. In the midst of battle, you need a friend. Sometimes you need to be reminded of your purpose so that you can stay strong in the fight of life.

Very recently, I felt as though I was in hand-to-hand combat. Not only entering into a verbal dispute over nonsense but also just the stress of where I work (at a school). I get stressed knowing the harsh realities many of the students have to face at their homes. I carry the burden home with me and I try not to but it's difficult when I have to look into the eyes of these students and show them compassion knowing that's really all I can offer. It makes me sad. I often wonder why God has me there, especially when I feel unappreciated and incapable of really making a difference.

Today my rainbow came to me in two forms: a co-worker that I've found to be a true blue friend for life and my husband. My husband came to my job when I asked him to pick me up. He helped me breathe and get myself together. Then, my co-worker encouraged me and reminded me that God does have a great purpose for me at the school, no matter what challenges I face in the form of people. She told me that I am important and am not a second-class citizen. She made me smile (and cry!) and feel good about myself.

That's what true Christianity is about: putting aside yourself and allowing God to use you for His purpose. Are you willing to be an encouragement to someone else? There's a song that says: "Sometimes you have to encourage yourself." Well there are also times when you can't encourage yourself and you need someone else to help. Today, if given the opportunity, encourage someone who needs it. I'm sure you won't have to look far.

Love,

Kelli Raí

The Power of Prayer

James 5:13, 17-18 (NLT) "Are any of you suffering hardships? You should pray. Are any of you happy? You should sing praises. Elijah was as human as we are, and yet when he prayed earnestly that no rain would fall, none fell for three and a half years! Then, when he prayed again, the sky sent down rain and the earth began to yield its crops."

Hello Beautifuls,

It seems that financial matters are brought to the forefront during the holiday season. There are class parties at school to which you have to donate food and/or money. There are extra groceries to be bought to make cookies and extravagant holiday meals. And not to mention all the gifts you want to buy for the people you love. December, alone, will make you think about your bank account. Although hardships don't always equal money, these days it does for many people. This morning, I was led to the book of James chapter 5 and verse 13 stood out which asks the question, "Are any of you suffering hardships?" (Many of us can yell out, "YES!") The simple answer to that is to pray. Verses 17 and 18 go on to show how Elijah demonstrated the power of prayer.

The point of praying about your hardships is not necessarily to ask for money or for things. How about praying for peace during your hardship or for a happy heart so that you can sing praises in spite of what you see? Pray to see the light at the end of your tunnel. Pray for an increase of faith so that you won't worry about the circumstances you are facing. There is real power in prayer. Prayer is talking to God. He has all power. More than that, He *wants* us to communicate with Him! When we don't pray, we're not tapping into our greatest resource!

We need to pray during hardships and good times. We need to praise during hardships and during good times. Now is the time to identify those things for which we are thankful. I'm ultimately thankful Jesus loved us enough to come to earth in human form to save our lives. I'm thankful that He's coming back to get us so that we can go to Heaven with Him. When I think of those things, everything else pales in comparison. I don't care about money or gifts or food or issues; I know that He will take care of all my needs because I've asked Him to do just that. Pray and ask Him for guidance. Even if you don't know what to say, He knows what you are feeling and what you're going through. Just take the first step in going to Him and He can take over from there.

Love,

Kelli Raí

Refresh

Psalm 51:10 (KJV) "Create in me a clean heart, O God; and renew a right spirit within me."

Hello Beautifuls,

Since this New Year has started, have you been bombarded with the idea of resolutions and new beginnings? I usually don't make New Year's resolutions. I'm all about new beginnings but I try to let God guide that part. When I need to make a new beginning, for the most part, I keep it to myself. I don't save a new beginning for the beginning of the year; I do it when it needs to happen no matter what time of year it happens to be. But at the beginning of this new year of 2009, I find that I have to renew my relationship with God.

I have fallen way off course with worship and reading God's word. I pray in the morning and during the day, but the TV puts me to bed. I pray as I drift to sleep sometimes. God calls for more. He's a jealous God and wants nothing keeping me from Him. So, I'm renewing my faith and my worship life. I find that when I'm under attack and I haven't been communicating well with God, I have no ammunition to fight. If my faith is weak, there's no way I can face hand-to-hand combat. I have been under attack. And in spite of my weakened state, God has kept me. I'm bruised and battered, so to speak, but I'm blessed with the opportunity to have Him fight my battles. All I have to do is ask and give it to Him.

It's important to keep your relationship with God fresh, not only because of tests and trials and attacks, but also just because God loves you. He created us for relationships... for a relationship with Him. You need a good connection with Him to thrive in the relationships that you have with your spouse, friends, and loved ones. We really benefit when we submit ourselves to God because He is there for you in every aspect of your life. He cares about all your cares.

Do you need a new beginning? Just start it. Don't delay simply because you don't want to be a part of a cliché. Do you need a refresher? Go get it! Are you already good in your maintenance? Then share your blessings with another.

Love,

Kelli Raí

Brighten the Corner

John 3:17 (NLT) "God sent his Son into the world not to judge the world, but to save the world through him."

Hello Beautifuls,

This week, a recurring theme showed up in my conversations. The theme was denominations, and how Christians treat people who visit their churches. I've been to churches where I was greeted warmly and welcomed with open arms, and I've been to churches where no one spoke to me. It doesn't bother me much when church folk don't have much to say to me. And I find that I have to step out of my comfort zone to make others feel welcome and I try to make an effort to do so. But the fact that it's comfortable for me to keep to myself has no bearing on my feeling that I'm in a clique and others should feel privileged to be invited to visit.

Church is a place of worship. It's not a place to guard your territory (regular seats), to ostracize others (indignantly judge people's attire), or just hang with your clique (and not warmly receive others around you). Sometimes people who call themselves Christians don't act like a follower of Jesus Christ should. We're all human. But, if we truly are followers of Jesus, we're to treat people the way He treated others. His main goal was to save, heal, and forgive.

Does your behavior show that you want someone's life to be saved, for their ills to be healed, and their sins forgiven? If it does, FABULOUS! I'd love to go to a church and encounter someone like you. If it doesn't, then it's time to do some "housecleaning." Let's all look at others through God's eyes, as difficult as that may be. Let's be loving, caring, forgiving, warm, and welcoming. Let's do our part to allow God to shine through us.

Love,

Kelli Raí

Hope for the Hopeless

Psalm 25:5 (NLT) "Lead me by your truth and teach me, for you are the God who saves me. All day long I put my hope in you."

Hello Beautifuls,

This week, I heard a terrible story about a family found slain in their home. As more facts of the story came to light, it was found that the father and mother had a murder/suicide pact because they had lost their jobs. They killed their children because they didn't want strangers to raise their children. These parents, leaders of their household, lost all hope because they were laid off. The newscaster reported suicide because of job loss is a growing trend. As much as this saddened me, I am blessed to know that there is always hope in Jesus. If you love Him, you have hope. You've got to trust him.

An important thing that God wants you to know is this: no situation you <u>ever</u> encounter is hopeless. He is God of all and He has the power to do anything.

Years ago I felt hopeless because of some health concerns I had to face. God brought me through that time and healed my body and my mind. And at the end of 2007, I lost my job, but as my job was being phased out, God blessed me with work at my children's school. Though I'm not making anything close to what I used to make, we are still very blessed financially. God always makes a way for us when things seem bleak. He has always taken care of us. God doesn't only go all out for us in our finances but in many other ways too: medically, legally, psychologically, etc.

I pray that all of you have hope in the Lord. If you have tried everything else to no avail, you won't be wasting your time trying God. Don't cut yourself short. God loves you and He wants you to survive. You are alive now for a reason because there is a very real purpose for your life. Try Him out. The peace of mind is worth it!

Love,

Kelli Raí

Brokenness

Psalm 34:18 (NLT) "The Lord is close to the broken hearted; he rescues those whose spirits are crushed."

Hello Beautifuls,

Has your heart ever been broken? Have you ever felt as if your spirit was broken? If not, you more than likely know someone who has. There are so many broken people in this world. There may even be someone close to you (or that you interact with) that is experiencing negative brokenness; but the person either hides it or doesn't recognize it. Whether you are aware of it or not, broken people need to be healed. They need to feel God's presence.

Psalm 34:18 talks about the fact that God is close to the brokenhearted and those whose spirits are crushed. Most people feel the furthest from God when they are sad, depressed, angry, grieving, and/or ruined inside. They feel so isolated and alone that they don't recognize that Jesus is right there! He's holding them in His loving arms. He wants them to give Him their heaviness so that they can heal.

It is good for us to show compassion and love to others. Sometimes God uses us to help someone who is hurting to feel His presence. Sometimes He uses us to prove to His hurting child that He really does love them. So, today, be a vessel for God. Be willing to be used by Him. Pray for those you know are hurting and allow God to shine through you for them. If it is you that is hurting, know that you are not alone. Jesus is with you right now.

Love,

Kelli Raí

Let God!

Exodus 15:2 (NLT) *"The Lord is my strength and my song; he has given me victory. This is my God, and I will praise him—my father's God, and I will exalt him!"*

Hello Beautifuls,

Have you ever gone through a challenge, trial, or test that just really took you for a loop? Sometimes we are faced with great challenges that make us wonder why we have to take it on and how on earth we will conquer it. I'm here today to tell you that God doesn't allow things to come into our path that we can't handle. He doesn't give us tests that we can't pass. As a matter of fact, more than likely, we freak out because we're so used to handling things ourselves and realize that only God can help us through this time. We're afraid to let go and let God handle the challenge. A big part of handling the challenge is giving it to God.

One morning earlier this week, I was awakened by a song sung by DeWayne Woods that says, "As soon as I stop worrying, worrying how the story ends, I let go and I let God; let God have His way." That song really spoke to me. I often find myself worrying about how an issue is going to play out instead of trusting that God will just handle it His way, if I let Him. The end of the song repeats, "Let go... let God." That's the ultimate answer! Difficult sometimes but it *is* the answer.

Then this morning I was awakened by a song sung by Maurette Brown Clark that says, "It ain't over until God says it's over; it ain't over until God says it's done; it ain't over until God says it's over; keep fighting until the victory is won." That song blessed me. It gave me encouragement to keep fighting until I get the victory. The victory is guaranteed when I have faith and trust in the Lord.

If you are going through some trial, know that you can win. You really can! Know that God will give you all the strength you need; all you need to do is ask Him. Your victory is guaranteed because Jesus died for you. But to make it through this particular challenge that you may be facing, give it to Him. It's not gonna be over until He says it's over. Keep fighting. Keep your faith. I know it may seem very difficult at times. Pray and let Him know that it's hard... it's too much... and then listen to Him tell you that you can make it with His strength. You can talk to God about anything. He wants to hear from you and talk to you. He doesn't want you to be stressed about anything.

Today, I challenge you to find the strength to let God handle your challenge, trial, or test. If you know someone who's going through, be their support and lift them up in prayer.

Love,

Kelli Raí

Take Time to Make Time

Psalm 46:10, 11 (NLT) "Be still and know that I am God! I will be honored by every nation. I will be honored throughout the world. The Lord of Heaven's Armies is here among us; the God of Israel is our fortress."

Hello Beautifuls,

I experienced a wonderful blessing the other evening. Driving home from the grocery store, I stopped at a red light and happened to notice the sky.

Directly over the town was a thick, dark gray cloud cover. Far off in the distance I could see the setting sun at the edge of the sky. The clouds out there were pink and orange and the sky was yellow. While I was taking in the beauty of it all, I heard the Lord say to me, "I'm still here. I'm here. Take time to notice me."

Whatever is going on in your life; whatever is clouding your mind, you should take time to notice God. You should spend time with Him. Welcome His presence into your life. Accept His peace to put order to your chaos. It's not His will that we should be rushing around in confusion. He wants to order our steps. Take time to notice His presence. He's still here no matter how you feel… no matter your circumstances… He's still here! He's here to comfort you, to guide you, to teach you, to bless you, to love you, and so much more.

This week, I challenge you to make time for God. Spend some time relishing in His presence. Welcome Him into your life.

Love,

Kelli Raí

Nourishment

Luke 10: 38-42 (NLT) "As Jesus and the disciples continued on their way to Jerusalem, they came to a certain village where a woman named Martha welcomed him into her home. Her sister, Mary, sat at the Lord's feet, listening to what he taught. But Martha was distracted by the big dinner she was preparing. She came to Jesus and said, "Lord, doesn't it seem unfair to you that my sister just sits here while I do all the work? Tell her to come and help me." But the Lord said to her, "My dear Martha, you are worried and upset over all these details! There is only one thing worth being concerned about. Mary has discovered it, and it will not be taken away from her."

Hello Beautifuls,

Recently, I was thinking about the fact that many of us don't take care of ourselves the way we should. So often we get caught up in caring for others that we don't notice that our energy source is depleted until we're completely burnt out. Mentally, physically, and spiritually we give and give without replenishing what's gone from us. Without proper rest, eating habits, exercise habits, and personal worship, we'll burn out faster than we realize.

Let's look at the sisters, Mary and Martha, who loved Jesus. Mary would sit spellbound at Jesus' feet while Martha worked her fingers to the bone between the dining room and the kitchen making sure her visitors were taken care of and fed. Mary was more interested in being fed spiritually by Jesus: caught up in every word he uttered... drinking it all in. When Martha realized she was doing too much by herself, she complained to Jesus. Jesus had to set her straight. It was better that they *all* sit at His feet than work too hard and complain. Food would be there. Water would be there. Personal time with Jesus would not always be there. Translation: feast on spiritual food then go out replenished to bless another.

It's so important to take care of yourself before caring for others. What sense does it make to create a feast for folks while you are malnourished and faint in the kitchen? At that point, you'd have no strength to even present the meal. If you are in need, how can you effectively care for another? It is good to take personal time and get fed by the Father so that you can share Him with another. Making time to connect with God is essential to help you and those with whom you come in contact.

I challenge you this week to make *more time* for Jesus.

Love,

Kelli Raí

While We are Waiting

Job 13:15 (NKJV) "Though He slay me, yet will I trust Him. Even so, I will defend my own ways before Him."

Hello Beautifuls,

One morning, I walked across the street from my job to get coffee at 7-Eleven. While there I saw a man there with his granddaughter. He kept fussing at her for "touching everything" while he fixed up his coffee. She couldn't have been more than 6 years old. Immediately, my eyes welled up with tears, but I also smiled, because the two of them reminded me of my father with one of his grandchildren. The difference was my dad didn't drink coffee and I can't remember my dad *ever* chastising his grandbabies. In September and in October, I miss my dad more than any other time because it's the anniversary of his birth, sudden illness, and death.

Autumn used to be a time I dealt with depression and other symptoms of seasonal affective disorder from the time I was a child, from what I can remember. In 2007, God healed me of it. I tested it out by not being on meds when the end of September came and I had no symptoms for two years. Then, in September of 2009 the doctors discovered that my father was terminally ill and he passed away that October. Talk about God's mercy on me! Who knows what kind of stress I would have been under suffering from S.A.D. and dealing with such trauma as my family experienced! I may not have been able to handle what was required of me as an adult daughter and sister at that time. I'm thankful that God healed me when he did. I believe that he looked down the path of my life and saw the possibility of what could be and spared me.

I trust God. I think that everything happens for a reason, and everything happens in its time. Yes, I miss my father a great deal. Yes, I have bouts of grief, but nothing like when it was fresh. God was merciful throughout the entire ordeal and he continues to be merciful.

I really meant for this message to be about allowing yourself and others to grieve in the way that they need to grieve. I wanted this message to be about how we should be gentle with ourselves and compassionate to others when it comes to dealing with loss. But, it turns out that this message is about God's mercy and trusting in Him. There have been so many sudden deaths in my circle. We ask God, "why?" His answer is to just blanket us with His love. Perhaps the answer will come when we can ask Him face to face.

While we're here, lets be loving and compassionate to others and ourselves. Let us give God the praise while our hearts break. Let us allow God to heal us and comfort us and draw us closer to Him. While we don't understand why things happen the way they do, let us allow God to cover us and guide us with every step we take each day. Don't give up. Don't despair. God hasn't left us, not for one minute.

Love,

Kelli Raí

He Won't Give Up on You

Nehemiah 9:16-17, 19-21 (NLT) [16] *"But our ancestors were proud and stubborn, and they paid no attention to your commands.* [17] *They refused to obey and did not remember the miracles you had done for them. Instead, they became stubborn and appointed a leader to take them back to their slavery in Egypt! But you are a God of forgiveness, gracious and merciful, slow to become angry, and rich in unfailing love. You did not abandon them...* [19] *"But in your great mercy you did not abandon them to die in the wilderness. The pillar of cloud still led them forward by day, and the pillar of fire showed them the way through the night.* [20] *You sent your good Spirit to instruct them, and you did not stop giving them manna from Heaven or water for their thirst.* [21] *For forty years you sustained them in the wilderness, and they lacked nothing. Their clothes did not wear out, and their feet did not swell!"*

Hello Beautifuls,

I'm so thankful for God's love. His unfailing love sustains me. When I am faced with a dilemma or situation that I can't handle on my own, God always comes through for me. He has increased my faith with His enduring love and consistency. I know that if I'm treated unfairly, God will make it right. And when I'm abandoned, He comforts me. Even when I've done wrong, He helps me and He encourages me to make it right. Through every hardship I've encountered, He's brought me through. He's healed my wounds. He does not allow suffering to last always.

As disobedient as His chosen people were, God was merciful and kept His promises to them. Though He was angered from time to time, He never gave up on His people. He had them walking around the wilderness for forty years, but their feet didn't swell, their clothes didn't wear out, He shielded them and led them, and he made sure they were fed. He provided all their needs. We may not be Israelites, but He's taking care of us too. He might take something away, but He will provide for your lack.

Be encouraged today that God won't fail you. If you've lost your job, your home, your loved one, your car…. Be assured that God will provide you with whatever you need. Do your best to trust that He will take care of you. Let Him have control of your situation. You have nothing to lose in trusting Him to help you. Take time to pray and worship, which should help you stay encouraged. He wants to help you. Let Him!

Love,

Kelli Raí

The Truth About Death

1 Corinthians 15:51, 52 (NLT) "But let me reveal to you a wonderful secret. We will not all die, but we will all be transformed! It will happen in a moment, in a blink of an eye, when the last trumpet is blown. For when the trumpet sounds, those who have died will be raised to live forever. And we who are living will also be transformed."

Hello Beautifuls,

I have been compelled to talk about a subject that I personally have a hard time dealing with. It seems that it's all around me. It seems to be happening more and more as time goes on. The subject is death. I was wondering if it was just my age... not that I'm old but I am getting older and I have friends of all ages. But it's not only older people dying; it's people of every age. It's not just people who've battled a long disease; it's people with short diseases, unexpected freak accidents, children, car accidents, etc.

People say that death is a part of life. That is a true statement. But death was not God's plan for our lives. His original plan was for us to live forever and dwell with Him. Adam and Eve had full access to the Tree of Life. It wasn't until our first parents ate of the Tree of the Knowledge of Good and Evil (the forbidden tree) that death became a part of our life cycle.

Death is sad. It leaves loved ones feeling empty, confused, lonely, and many other hopeless kinds of feelings. God is the only One who can fill voids and we don't always know to ask or how to ask God to fill this void of death. But He knows exactly how we feel and wants to fill up the empty places where our loved one once occupied in our lives.

The only light in the midst of this dark tunnel is that Jesus conquered death! Before sin entered the world, God had already in place the plan for our deliverance. Christ would come and pay the penalty for our personal and collective sins. He would die so we could live. This plan was for Jesus to come to earth in human form, live a sinless life, die for our sins (be our sacrificial lamb), rise again, and return to Heaven. He did all of those things. What love; what matchless love!!!

Though death leaves us feeling hopeless, we do have hope! Those that are in Christ who die will live again! He will raise them from the dead when He comes again so that we can live in Heaven with Him; then inhabit the New Jerusalem (see Revelation 20 and 21). Our job is not to worry if our loved one was Christian enough; we just need to have faith that God knows all, and keep on living.

Don't let the death of a loved one defeat you. As difficult as it may be to recover, rest assured that death will one day be obliterated when Jesus comes again. We have to keep on living, keep on praying, keep on worshiping, and keep on keeping on, in the meantime. Call on the Holy Spirit to be your Comfort and to fill the void that you feel in the center of your being. God knows how difficult death is and He wants you to go to Him for strength and endurance. You are never alone. You are never alone. He cares for you. He loves you more than anyone ever could. He will be your peace. He is right there next to you. Let Him carry you through your difficulty.

Love,

Kelli Raí

Be a Vessel

Acts 9:15 (KJV) "But the Lord said unto him, Go thy way: for he is a chosen vessel unto me, to bear my name before the Gentiles, and kings, and the children of Israel:"

Hello Beautifuls,

I've found that many of the "happymails" that I've sent out are about God using us for the benefit of others; about how we should allow God to use us. It is a powerful blessing to be chosen by God to be used by Him to speak to another person for His purpose. This is yet another message about the same thing. It's so important to ask Him to cleanse us so that He can dwell within us. When that happens He can then shine through us. When He shines through, people stop seeing you, and they see the beauty of the Lord. It is life saving and life changing.

A week ago, I was in the bank and the lady behind me was talking about how humid it was outside. I smiled and agreed. Then she mentioned that she really liked my hair and our small talk turned to hair. That hair talk went into how she was happy that she still has her hair, even though she's started chemo. I said, "Well that is such a blessing!" Then I was moved to ask her name; she said, "Gwen." I said, "Gwen, you will be in my prayers." She said thank you. We moved on. I finished my business, and as I left I approached her and said, "Gwen, I will be praying for you." She said, "Thank you. Let me give you a hug." We embraced and I walked to the car through a mist that filled my eyes. I really needed that hug. I truly believe God had me speak to her to encourage her through her fight for life. In turn He blessed me in that whole exchange. Still brings tears to my eyes.

I'm so thankful that He chose to use this unworthy, wayward, rebellious girl to simply say with a sincere heart, "I will pray for you," to a woman in need of it. And I'm still praying for the Gwen that I met in the bank. I'm praying for Mike. I'm praying for Pat. I'm probably praying for you too, if you've asked it of me. I'm a believer that prayer changes things: weeping to joy, death to life, mourning to dancing, chaos to peacefulness, and confusion to understanding. I want to be God's vessel: full of Him to be a blessing for someone else.

Last summer (2008) I had the privilege of sitting at my Aunt Gwen's (a different Gwen) bedside as she withered from the effects of cancer. The Lord blessed me with the gift of praying with her, singing to her, laughing with her, and eating with her at the end of her colorful life. He chose to use me to bring her a little happiness in the midst of death. What a special, special gift!

I challenge you to let Him into your heart, let Him cleanse you then shine through you. You won't regret it. It is one of the best blessings you will experience: to serve another so that God can be glorified. Be willing to be a vessel for Him.

Love,

Kelli Raí

Escape into Faithfulness

***1 Corinthians 10:13 (NLT)** "The temptations in your life are no different from what others experience. And God is faithful. He will not allow the temptation to be more than you can stand. When you are tempted, he will show you a way out so that you can endure."*

Hello Beautifuls,

Isn't it such a blessing to know that God is faithful? We fail Him all the time but He never lets us down. I have never known Him to let anyone down. Even when we face temptation, He provides a way of escape so that we can endure! We need that escape as time winds up and demons work more overtime than ever before to get us to fall and leave Jesus. One thing that should help us focus is the closeness of the second coming.

Jesus is coming. You can look around and see the signs. More people are dying than ever before: new diseases are appearing; more wars (and rumors of wars); the signs that Jesus mentioned in the gospels have already taken place; we're here waiting for Him to return while we live out our lives.

What are you doing while you wait? I recently heard a pastor speak at a funeral about time: what are you doing with your time? Are you helping someone who needs help? Are you giving a genuine smile to someone in your path? Are you missing the opportunities to spend time worshipping and meditating on Jesus? Are you helping someone else get to Heaven? Are you being faithful and walking right?

It pays to take time to do what God would have you do. It makes sense to even be willing to do whatever God wants you to do at anytime. One way to increase your faith is to take the time to be faithful. At those times when you find yourself in a quandary, you're being shaken a little to be drawn to Him again. He wants you to trust Him, not to look all around but just to Him for your help and salvation.

Don't fall into the temptation of not taking time out for God. Your way of escape is to worship. Don't fall into the temptation of selfishness. Your way of escape is to help someone else – even if it's just a smile. Remember that God has a purpose for your life and it's up to you to seek it out in Him. Be willing to be his vessel.

Love,

Kelli Raí

I Can!

Philippians 4:13 (KJV) "I can do all things through Christ who strengtheneth me."

Hello Beautifuls,

I saw a news program story about a young man who was in a swimming accident. He dove into a wave and hit a sand bar. Instantly, he was paralyzed from the neck down. The whole experience was devastating to him and his girlfriend. The young man didn't give up on being able to walk again, though all the doctors he came into contact with told him that he'd never walk again. His hope was heightened when he got in touch with the same doctor who worked with Christopher Reeves. She told him that there was definitely hope for him.

Because he had great determination, he is now able to walk with a walker, three years after his accident. He stated that he knows one day he'll walk out of his rehab center without the walker. He and his wife opened a rehab center in California that promotes the kind of work that helps those who suffer paralysis to walk again. They want to help others achieve full health again. They want others to have hope.

We can look at this story, which is absent of talk about God, and think that by sheer will, he's achieved many great accomplishments to get back to health. I would urge you to look deeper and know that you can do more, accomplish anything, and achieve anything through Christ who will give you the strength to do so! Not only can you have your health restored, but you can also be successful in life; you can achieve your goals, you can help others, you can live the life that God would have you live. Jesus will give you the strength and the will that you need to get to where you need to be.

So don't get caught up in "I can't". In Jesus you can say, "I can"! You can lose the weight; you can go back to school and graduate; you can get that job; you can raise your kids right; you can learn to cook; you can stop smoking; you can stop drinking; you can stop doing drugs; you can stop overeating; you can, you can, you can!!! Submit your will to the Lord and let Him guide your path.

I challenge you today to say, "I CAN!"

Love,

Kelli Raí

He Forgives Mistakes

Romans 5:15-17 (NLT) *"But there is a great difference between Adam's sin and God's gracious gift. For the sin of this one man, Adam, brought death to many. But even greater is God's wonderful grace and his gift of forgiveness to many through this other man, Jesus Christ. And the result of God's gracious gift is very different from the result of that one man's sin. For Adam's sin led to condemnation, but God's free gift leads to our being made right with God, even though we are guilty of many sins. For the sin of this one man, Adam, caused death to rule over many. But even greater is God's wonderful grace and his gift of righteousness, for all who receive it will live in triumph over sin and death through this one man, Jesus Christ."*

Hello Beautifuls,

Have you ever made a horrible mistake that couldn't be undone? What kind of attitude did you have? Were you sorrowful, trying to fix your mistake or did you act like you didn't care and just left the mess as it was?

I make mistakes all the time. I'm constantly worried that day-to-day I could be making mistakes that will cause my kids to need therapy later in life. But as humans we will make mistakes in life. No one is perfect. And when we do make mistakes, we must do our part to make things right again, whatever that may be.

Sometimes we make horrible sinful mistakes, the kind that make us wonder if God would ever truly forgive us and keep us as His children. The first way to make it right is to go to God and confess it to Him. We must then ask for forgiveness. We also must do the work to never make the mistake again. This involves leaning on God's strength to keep on the path He has for us. It also involves denying ourselves of the sinful indulgence we crave. If God leads us to confess to someone we sinned against, then we must also do that. God doesn't put our sins out in the open when we are committed to not repeat the mistakes and are leaning wholly on Him to be right in Him.

I recently read that someone was questioning whether God truly accepted us as His children because we tend to mess up so much. The pastor this person asked gave this explanation: he has a dog that is well trained, loyal and obedient. He also has a baby who makes a mess, has food all over him, and tears things up every chance he gets. Who will take his legacy, the dog or the baby? The answer is the baby.

God is invested in us, no matter how much we mess up, how many mistakes we make, or how much chaos we cause. He loves us and doesn't want us to mess up but knows that we may just do that. In those times He is still available to us to forgive and make the wrongs right.

Trust in the LORD today. Ask Him into your heart. Ask Him to show you the way to His righteousness and commit yourself to stay in His care. He can make order out of chaos. He is God.

Love,

Kelli Raí

He is Still Here

Psalm 13 (NLT) "O Lord, how long will you forget me? Forever? How long will you look the other way? How long must I struggle with anguish in my soul, with sorrow in my heart every day? How long will my enemies have the upper hand? Turn and answer me, O Lord my God! Restore the sparkle to my eyes, or I will die. Don't let my enemies gloat, saying, "We have defeated him!" Don't let them rejoice at my downfall. But I trust in your unfailing love. I will rejoice because you have rescued me. I will sing to the Lord because he is good to me."

Hello Beautifuls,

Lately I've been in such a rut: feeling low and in an odd mood. Intellectually, I know that God is with me and He loves me, but I've been feeling like David did in the beginning of the passage of Psalm 13: that maybe God had forgotten me and I didn't want the pain of feeling His absence for too much longer. But even in the midst of my rut, God kept sending me messages through my loved ones. I had a long talk with my father who kept stressing, "I know the Lord loves *you*, Kelli!" Even though each morning I awoke with praise songs on my mind, or when I asked God to make a way for me to minister and get a little extra income, He opened doors and made the way, I felt disconnected. He was still there communicating with me but I was standing in my own way.

I felt far from God even though God wasn't far from me. I felt like saying, "Restore the sparkle to my eyes, or I will die." I hate feeling sad. I hate the feeling of desperation. I had to realize that it wasn't that God was far from me, but that I was keeping myself from Him. I wasn't giving Him all of me; I was only giving Him parts of me. If you're only going to half step with God, you will definitely feel it. It's only when you give yourself to Him fully that you can experience the full peace of the joy of His salvation.

I dedicated myself to God again when I realized that I'd been keeping myself from Him. When I did that, I had such a feeling of peace and a knowing that He would take care of all my problems. I was scared to share it because I thought maybe whomever I told would think negatively of my experience. But I'm here to say that I went to God with my problems and after my season of prayer I had a knowing that He would take care of me and provide all my needs... even fix the messes that I'd made. I wasn't worried anymore.

If you ever find yourself feeling far from God, keep praying. Keep holding on to the knowledge that God will take care of you and that He loves you. Cling to His promises. He will guide you to what He wants you to do. Be willing to obey Him. He knows what's best.

Love,

Kelli Raí

Patiently Waiting for an Answer

Psalm 27:14 (NLT) "Wait patiently for the Lord. Be brave and courageous. Yes, wait patiently for the Lord."

Hello Beautifuls,

I woke up yesterday morning with the song, "I Need Thee" playing in my mind. Not the hymn but the song I used to sing with the group *Grace*. I realize more and more daily that I'm in need of God at all times. I'm helpless and powerless without Him. He is God. In most situations, only He can help fix the problem. We humans don't control anything but how we act and react when things arise.

Good friends of mine just experienced a miracle. They had lost something that would cost a great deal for them to replace. The last time I was with them, I had a strong feeling they would get back what they lost but I didn't mention it to them. Sure enough, what they had lost was recovered, after months of being without it. God was present in that situation: from the time it was lost until it was found. A non-believer would say: "Oh, God doesn't care about our small matters! He's not a lost-and-found!" But if you look a little deeper, you will see the miracle. They didn't have to spend the money (that could be better used elsewhere) to replace it. Perhaps a horrible incident was avoided during the time they waited to get it back. And their faith that God would see them through was being tested. (They passed that test.)

Sometimes when we pray about things, we have to wait. For some things, you have to wait months or years... for others maybe seconds or weeks. God doesn't always say "yes"... sometimes He says "no" or "wait". In the meantime, while you wait on the His answer, what kind of attitude will you have? Will you fervently seek out the Lord's will? Will you trust Him to work it out in His way since He knows what's best? Will you accept what He allows? Will you use the situation to draw you closer to Him and better your relationship with Him?

God does care about our cares. He created us in His image: tiny beings that can't be detected from light years away. He created us and longs to abide in us and have us dwell in His light for eternity. He works miracles even today. He healed me completely of my infirmity that I'd endured for years. He wants to help you too.

Today, I challenge you to realize your need for God and submit yourself to Him. Doing this will help you increase your faith in Him. When your faith increases, your bond with Him gets stronger. When your bond with God is stronger, you are better able face anything that comes your way.

Love,

Kelli Raí

A Place of Refuge

Psalm 62:7, 8 (NLT) "My victory and honor come from God alone. He is my refuge, a rock where no enemy can reach me. O my people, trust in him at all times. Pour out your heart to him, for God is our refuge."

Hello Beautifuls,

Wednesday evening, I was compelled to fill my evening with praise and worship because I was made aware that the enemy has waged war on my household. When discouragement enters my home, that's a sign of war and I have to be ready to fight with all my ammunition: praise, worship, fasting, and praying!

The theme God presented to me was that He is a place of refuge, our fortress of safety. My children's Sabbath school lesson talked about how in Moses' day, God had him set up cities of refuge for those people in need of fair trials, because not everything is in black and white. Back then, the law was "eye for an eye," but that rule gave no room for a gray area. So God had these cities of refuge set up and if a person made it to a city of refuge before the city's gates closed, they were more than likely welcomed to stay there until their trial was heard. The priest there decided who could stay. Refugees were safe as long as they stayed inside the city's walls. If they were to leave, they were in danger of being harmed by anyone looking for them. Some people had to spend their lives in these cities of refuge.

After that lesson, I was led to sing some hymns that fell under the heading "Faith and Trust." On one of the hymns, the Bible passage given was Psalm 61. There it talked about God being our refuge. I was then led to Psalm 62 that carried the same sentiments. I'm so blessed and thankful that God led me in worship and revealed Himself to me as my place of refuge, OUR place of refuge. I was so filled that I had to wake up my husband and share it with him.

Today I challenge you to put your faith and trust in the Lord. Know that He is your place of refuge and that He will also fight for you. He is your protector, fortress, safe dwelling, doctor, lawyer, etc. If you stay in Him, you will be well taken care of.

Love,

Kelli Raí

He's More Powerful Than...

Job 42:1 (NLT) "Then Job replied to the LORD: 'I know that you can do anything, and no one can stop you.'"

Hello Beautifuls,

When I fasted with my sisters when my dad was ill, God led me to read Job 38-42. In this passage God challenges Job after Job's rounds with his friends on whether or not his sinfulness brought on his illness and misfortune. God reminded Job of His power, might, and capabilities as God. He proved His Godliness to Job. At the end, Job could only reply with humility.

Take a few minutes to read Job 38-41. This passage tells us that God is all-powerful. We can get so caught up in the bad things that happen to us. And, yes, when it rains it pours. I'm a witness to that. But God's power and might outweigh any circumstance we could ever face! When we get through the challenges presented to us, we can sigh and say, "Wow, I made it with God's help." What good does it do to worry and complain?

As hard as it can be, we must continually put our cares in God's hands. We don't have the power to tell the wind where to blow and whether to be hot or cold; God does. We don't have the ability to stop time or walk on water; God does. We don't have the power to make stars fall; turn the moon to blood, or to turn the sun black; God does. He is All-Powerful, Omniscient, Omnipresent and He is in control. So why not put your cares in the hands of the One Who cares for you? The One Who created life? The One Who the winds and seas obey? Why not put your life in the hands of the One Who created you? He looked down the line before time and saw you at this day, this time and knew you were to be exactly where you are. Why not trust Him to take care of you? He already knows what you're facing.

Today, I challenge you to accept His power and ask Him to use it to take you through your rough times and still be there through the easy times. The rough times won't last always, and you'll still want His presence with the trouble is over. Trust Him to keep you always.

Love,

Kelli Raí

When He Cometh

Matthew 27:50-53 (NLT) "Then Jesus shouted out again, and he released his spirit. At that moment the curtain in the sanctuary of the Temple was torn in two, from top to bottom. The earth shook, rocks split apart, and tombs opened. The bodies of many godly men and women who had died were raised from the dead. They left the cemetery after Jesus' resurrection, went into the holy city of Jerusalem, and appeared to many people."

Hello Beautifuls,

Have you ever had a loved one die? If so, you know the depth of pain that is felt. You know the ache that can exist in your soul... you know the feeling of having a void inside that you couldn't ever fill. I lost my father on October 22, 2009. I can't begin to tell you the kind of grief I have been experiencing. And I can't imagine the kind of grief my mother is experiencing. I don't even know what my sisters are feeling but I have an idea.

In the midst of trauma and pain, one tends to wonder if God cares. One tends to wonder why this horrible feeling exists and why they must endure it. But I know God cares that we're grieving. I know He feels my pain. He loves me, us. He Himself has experienced this pain. Jesus' dear friend Lazarus died. Jesus wept. The dictionary defines weep as, "to express grief, sorrow, or any overpowering emotion by shedding tears." That means Jesus was definitely hurting for the loss of His friend even though He was to resurrect him. God the Father experienced this pain when His only begotten Son was tortured and crucified. This pain was evidenced in what the Word tells us in Matthew 27:50-53. My God knows my pain. So He sent the Comforter to surround us with His presence. He has the power to fill this void.

I know that we will survive this. God knows everything. My (then 9-year-old) daughter Zoie said to us after the news of my father's passing, "God knows what He's doing even if we don't know why." There's a reason why we've had this experience. While in the hospital, Daddy said that his illness wasn't about him, but was for others around him. That we are to take this time for introspection and get right with God.

Sooner than we expect, Jesus will return to take His righteous home. I believe Daddy was ready when he went to sleep. I want to be caught up with Jesus when he comes. I want all my loved ones to go to Heaven when Jesus comes. I challenge you today, because I love you, to get right with the Lord. Cast aside whatever is keeping you from Him. Ask Him to help you. Be ready when Jesus comes. Tomorrow isn't promised. Do it today... right now!

Love,

Kelli Raí

Angels Watchin' Over Me, My Lord

Psalm 91:11 (NLT) *"For he will order his angels to protect you wherever you go. They will hold you up with their hands so you won't even hurt your foot on a stone."*

Hello Beautifuls,

On my return flight to DC after my father's funeral, I read the book In The Presence Of Angels by E. Lonnie Melashenko and Timothy E. Crosby. I found the book in my dad's home office and was moved to read it. Oh, what a joy and comfort it brought to me. It really reaffirmed my faith that God cares about me and that He sends His angels to protect, comfort, help, and give guidance. I truly believe that while there are demons aiming to kill and destroy us, there are Heavenly angels surrounding us, keeping us safe who believe and have faith in the Lord. The book showed that they also appear to us at times in human form and angelic form, when God deems it necessary, just like in the Bible days.

While reading the book, I was reminded of the time when an angel awoke me to have a morning conversation the Lord. This was during a rough time in my life and I was seeking God daily through fasting and prayer. My children and I were staying with some friends of ours while the bathroom and kitchen at our house were being renovated. A good friend of mine, LaFese, was also fasting with me. When we talked one evening, we decided to get up and pray at 5:00 the next morning. Well, when morning came, I was exhausted and I didn't want to get up. So when my alarm went off at 4:45 a.m., I set it for 6:00 a.m., because I wanted to sleep. As soon as I fell back to sleep, I heard my girlfriend's dog barking and jumping up on the slatted door in the laundry room next to the room I where my children and I were sleeping. I yelled to the dog to stop it. He kept on barking and jumping on the slatted doors, so I got up. When I walked out of my room, there was no sound and no dog. The dog was not in the laundry room but upstairs in the garage and couldn't be heard in the house from the garage. God sent His angel to awaken me so that He could commune with me that day.

At the same time, miles away, LaFese had a similar experience. Teenagers running up and down the hallway of her apartment building awakened her. They were really, really loud, but normally she wasn't awakened by noises in the hallway. When she finally got up and opened her door, she heard scurrying feet down the stairs. It sounded like they were right beneath her at this point and she heard someone say, "Ooh, it's cold out here!" And then an apartment door opened and closed. To her knowledge, no teens lived on that floor. It was also a very warm morning. Confused, she walked back to her room and prayed. Those had to be angels awakening her to talk to Jesus. He wanted us to keep our appointment with Him.

These are the last days and God is moving. He wants our attention so that we will be ready when He comes. He also wants us to be strong enough to stand in the time right before He comes. He still sends His angels to fight for us, protect us, give us messages, get our attention, help us, and comfort us. Praise God that He is interested enough in us that He would send personal messengers to do His bidding.

I challenge you, today, to open your heart to the Lord today and let Him guide and strengthen you. Let Him cleanse and save you. Be ready to stand for Him and to go with Him to Heaven when He comes back to get us.

Love,
Kelli Raí

Determination

Philippians 3:14 (NLT) "I press on to reach the end of the race and receive the Heavenly prize for which God, through Christ Jesus, is calling us."

Hello Beautifuls,

Has your life always been perfect? Or have you had the experience of something bad happening to you? And if something bad has happened to you, how did you react? Did you get up and pick things up again so that your life could come back together? Were you so blown by what happened that you didn't know how to go on?

Sometimes when bad things happen, people tend to stop doing things they normally do. They stop functioning in the positive. When trouble comes some people turn away from God and start to just exist. They lose faith that God, our loving God of mercy, will bring us through the trial. This happening is more commonly called depression. Sometimes it seems that it can't be controlled... but God can help us in any circumstance. He can do anything.

Tragedy struck my life, and I didn't know if I could come back from the blow. But I decided that I'm not going stop my life because of it. I can't stop. I have to keep on doing the work God has for me to do. I'm going to keep on raising my children the way God would have me raise them. I'm still going to work where God wants me to work. I'm not going to stop because I can't let the devil have the victory over my life. So I'm not going to stop. I have to fight to stay on course. Even though I may have to take a moment and breathe and scream and cry and ask why, at the end of it, I must continue on the path.

I challenge you to keep on going. Keep going especially if life has you down. I challenge you to allow God to take you by the hand and lead you. Keep on going. Keep the Lord ever before you and just keep going.

Love,

Kelli Raí

Thought of Me Above All

***John 1:1-4, 14 (KJV)** "In the beginning was the Word, and the Word was with God, and the Word was God. The same was in the beginning with God. All things were made by him; and without him was not any thing made that was made. In him was life; and the life was the light of men.... And the Word was made flesh, and dwelt among us, (and we beheld his glory, the glory as of the only begotten of the Father,) full of grace and truth."*

Hello Beautifuls,

The Christmas season seems to be, at times, the rehearsed story of Christ's birth. But tonight it really resonated with me. Our God, our Mighty Creator became His creation... a vulnerable, poor, human baby. Oh, how the inhabitants of Heaven must have held their breath. It would seem that the earth would quake, the winds would howl, lightning would streak across the sky and thunder would roll. Instead was the beautiful sound of the angel choir singing praises. A bright star (probably an angel) guided the way for the wise men to find our Holy God. He was born to save us and give us salvation; not just for the people of His lifetime, but for those of us generations later.

My thoughts then went to His death, for He was born to die. When He died the earth *did* quake, winds *did* howl, lightning *did* streak across the sky and the thunder *did* roll. Dead people resurrected. Again, the inhabitants of Heaven must have held their breath. God the Father was, for the first time, separated from His only Son by sin.... He conquered death and the grave through resurrection and Salvation was fulfilled. Jesus is to come again to take us to Heaven, then we will later dwell in the New Jerusalem. I encourage you to take time to read Revelation.

I'm so humbled by the thought that my Wonderful Creator decided to become human to save my life. That He loves me so much and wanted so much to commune with me beyond eternity, He took the risk stepping down from Heaven and coming to earth to live a difficult life. He went toe to toe with the devil just for me. Why shouldn't I be willing to give my life to Him? Why am I not more inclined to do His will? Woe is me if I only meagerly attempt to follow Him and lose my salvation over an idiotic sin from which He is willing to redeem me.

I challenge you to take a deeper look at Jesus and not simply repeat the story. Allow yourself to really take in the depth of His actions on your behalf. I challenge you to have a closer walk with the Savior.

Love,

Kelli Raí

*Originally published in

Prayer of Thanksgiving

2 Timothy 2:11-13 (NLT) "This is a trustworthy saying: If we die with him, we also will live with him. If we endure hardship, we will reign with him. If we deny him, he will deny us. If we are unfaithful, he remains faithful, for he cannot deny who he is."

Hello Beautifuls,

I'd like to share a prayer with you instead of a message. The act of thanksgiving is a message. It's important to give thanks to God for all He has done, is doing, and will do for you and your family. Also it's important to give to others: give of your time, care, love, food, shelter, clothing... whatever God impresses upon you to give, you should give.

"Dear Jesus, I love you. I want more of You and less of me. When I'm in your presence, nothing else matters. I could lose every material thing I have, but if I have You, I know I'll be just fine. You didn't give me life for me to fail. Fight my battles, Lord. Take away my sin, Lord. Take care of everything, Lord. Let me just worship You. I love You. Thank You for loving me first, way before my time. You looked down the line before life existed and saw me. Thank You for seeing me. Thank You for planting me and growing me. I give my life, my everything to You. I give You my every care. Thank you for taking my burden. Amen."

Be blessed.

Love,

Kelli Raí

He will Come Through

Matthew 17:20 (NLT) "'You don't have enough faith," Jesus told them. "I tell you the truth, if you had faith even as small as a mustard seed, you could say to this mountain, 'Move from here to there,' and it would move. Nothing would be impossible.'"

Hello Beautifuls,

It seems that over and over again, I struggle when it comes to having blind faith. I have to remind myself of the times when God came through for me when I didn't know where provisions were going to come from. There are many instances that I can remember just to help build my confidence in knowing what God can and will do on my behalf. I remember when we were rejoicing in the fact that God provided exactly what Mykel, my oldest child, needed to re-enroll at her school for her senior year of high school. It was a true blessing and testament that God can do anything and will do what we need Him to do on our behalf.

Even so, I'm human and I soon found myself facing another mountain. Where was my faith? I was listening to a song on the way in to work one day that professes, "You are the God who can do miracles / You are the God who shall prevail / You are the God Who's able to keep me / You are the God who never fails . . ." (Anthony Brown). I could quote the entire song because each word speaks life into my spirit. How could I doubt God? I *know* He performs miracles and He has *never* failed me! So I started to cry while listening to this song that morning. I asked God to give me more evidence that He will come through for me.

(I work in Admissions at a Christian high school. I often end up witnessing to people interested in sending their children to school, who can't see a way to pay the tuition.)

When I arrived at work that day, the first conversation I had on the phone was with a new parent. I was returning her call and she indicated that she got an answer to her question the afternoon after she called the day before. But then she broke down crying, "It's so hard!" She went on to explain that she had gotten a new job then lost it when she needed at least two weeks to heal from falling down the stairs. Her employer fired her because they needed her to work and couldn't wait for her. Through her tears, she told me that she'd been praying and told God that she would pay whatever it took to send her daughter to our school. I got choked up while listening to her and I stopped her. I said, "lets change your prayer: change your prayer to, 'Lord, you blessed me with this child and You know how important Christian education is for her. Please supply our needs. You have all the money and you said you would take care of us. Please take care of this need.'" Then I prayed with her and encouraged her before we hung up. That situation was God making me reach down deep and step up for Him while He strengthens my faith once again. I had to minister to someone else while God ministered to me. He answered the prayer I whispered to Him while in the car.

My challenge for you is to allow God to increase your faith. He really can do anything. He is all-powerful and ever present. And while your faith is increased, share your story and pray for someone else.

Love,

Kelli Raí

Make Room

Luke 2:7 (KJV) *"And she brought forth her firstborn son, and wrapped him in swaddling clothes, and laid him in a manger, because there was no room for them in the inn."*

Hello Beautifuls,

Over the Christmas holiday, I was thinking about the hardship Jesus encountered before He was born. His earthly parents, Mary and Joseph, couldn't find a proper place for Mary to give birth to Jesus. Many turned them away before a stable used by animals was offered. He had very humble beginnings.

This impacted His ministry. His early life helped pave the way for how He lived His life and what He would preach: give to the poor; help the needy. In essence, these were a major part of His ministry. From His birth He encountered people turning Him away. He knew what it felt like to have someone turn away from Him. Jesus wanted to turn this around teach people compassion so that more people could have positive experiences that come from making room- provisions- for others.

I heard a song called "No Room" which talks about there not being any room for Jesus to come into the world. It made me think of how we don't make room for Him in our hearts, and we don't make room for Him in our lives. Too often we close ourselves off so that we can't even consider doing His service.

I challenge you to make room for Jesus. Make room for others. Make room in your schedule to do His service. Be willing to let Him use you.

Love,

Kelli Raí

Good Communication

Psalm 6:9 (KJV) "The LORD hath heard my supplication; the LORD will receive my prayer."

Hello Beautifuls,

Today I was reminded how important communication is in a relationship. Good communication helps people understand each other. In a marriage, good communication is key to help each person know how the other feels, what he or she is going through, or his or her way of thinking. It's important for couples to communicate about everything, I was once told. Talking about things that seem minor can make a difference in a relationship. For example, a person can feel resentful of their spouse for always turning off the TV when they fall asleep on the couch instead of waking them up and asking them to bed. Or the spouse can feel resentful if their spouse falls asleep in front of the TV every night. Things could easily be resolved in the beginning by having a simple conversation. "Honey, when I fall asleep in front of the TV, could you please wake me up?" or "Honey, it bothers me when you fall asleep in front of the TV every night, can we find an evening activity to do together some nights?"

Good communication with God is important, if we want our relationship with Him to grow and mature. It's not enough to go to church every Sabbath. We need to read our Bibles after praying for God's guidance in what He would have us learn from Him in His Word. We should study the Bible. We should engage in activities that draw us closer to Him. But most important is that we pray every day. My husband and I were telling our children one evening that they could talk to us about anything at all. We stressed the fact that they should not be scared to talk to us about what's going on with them. If they are having a problem, we can't be of any help to them unless they talk to us or ask us for help. It's similar with our relationship and communication with God.

He already knows what's going on with us, but He wants us to tell Him. We have to confess our sins and ask for forgiveness because if we don't, He can't cleanse us of our sins. He will not force Himself upon us. It's good for us to talk to Him about what's going on with us whether we are happy, sad, angry, confused, exhausted, elated, peaceful, etc. He always wants to hear from us. There is something freeing about talking things out. When you confess your sins, a weight is lifted. When you tell God about your pain and anguish, you can let go of it and receive His peace. He can do anything for us if we just ask... when our will is in line with His will. First Thessalonians 5:17 says "Pray without ceasing." That means that we should always be in communication with the Father.

I challenge you to spend some extra time talking to God. Not just before you go to sleep or when you wake up, but while you cook dinner, or while driving somewhere without the radio, or while you're conversing with a friend. Let your relationship with Him grow and bloom.

Love,

Kelli Raí

Trouble Sleeping

1 Samuel 3:1, 10 (NLT) "Meanwhile, the boy Samuel served the LORD by assisting Eli. Now in those days messages from the LORD were very rare, and visions were quite uncommon.... And the LORD came and called as before, 'Samuel! Samuel!' And Samuel replied, 'Speak, your servant is listening.'"

Hello Beautifuls,

Have you ever had trouble sleeping and had no idea why? Ever been awakened consistently at a specific time in the middle of the night for a few days in a row? God may be trying to have a conversation with you.

In the days before Israel had kings, there was a special boy named Samuel who was sent to live with the priest Eli. His mother dedicated him to the LORD because she'd longed to have a son and finally God blessed her with Samuel. She'd promised to give him to the priest so that he could live his life serving the LORD and with her keeping her promise, God blessed her with more children. So, this Samuel was special in that God chose to speak to him. He later became God's special prophet. God started speaking to Samuel in his childhood... in the middle of the night when everyone else was asleep. Eli recognized that God was awaking Samuel and he told him what to say, "Speak, your servant is listening."

God still speaks to us today. Not always giving us messages for others; sometimes He just wants to talk to us. He wants our full attention. What other time is better than when the house is sleeping and there are no other distractions... when you can clearly hear what He wants to say. If you are awakened in the middle of the night consistently and you have no sleeping disorder (smile), the LORD may just be wanting to commune with you. I've personally had this experience more than once. A couple times, I said in my mind, "Speak LORD your servant heareth," and I just tuned in to the LORD. I prayed and then listened. And He spoke to me.

The next time you are awakened and you have no idea why you are awake and can't go back to sleep, don't turn on the TV or a CD, pray. Your mind will stay at ease and you won't be over-stimulated so that you can have a restful sleep until you have to wake up.

Take time to talk **and** listen to God.

Love,

Kelli Raí

Be a Doer, Not Just a Believer

Hebrews 3:12-16 (NIrV) "Brothers and sisters, make sure that none of you has a sinful heart. Do not let an unbelieving heart turn you away from the living God. But build one another up every day. Do it as long as there is still time. Then none of you will become stubborn. You won't be fooled by sin's tricks. We belong to Christ if we hold firmly to the faith we had at first. But we must hold to it until the end. It has just been said, 'Listen to his voice today. If you hear it, don't be stubborn. You were stubborn when you opposed me.' Who were those who heard and refused to obey? Weren't they all the people Moses led out of Egypt?"

Hello Beautifuls,

One evening my son (then 8 years old) asked if he could read a passage for worship. The above passage is the one he picked. I was floored. I was amazed how God will use His babies to give an important message to us. If we would just step back sometimes and give our children some leeway (after having given previous instruction), God will use our children as His vessels.

I definitely needed to hear this passage. It made me look at myself: am I holding on to a sinful heart? Do I build up the believers in my household and my workplace daily? If I think someone is stubborn when it comes to Christianity, am I partially to blame because I haven't done my part? Am I holding on to the faith I had as a child when I was first baptized into the church? So many facets of who I need to be and hope to be are held in the given passage.

So, take a look at yourself. Are you holding yourself back from God? Are you standing in the way of someone else getting to God? What is the condition of your heart? Do you take time everyday to build up your brothers and sisters in the faith?   Are you as steadfast now as you were when you first believed?

I know; so many questions. But, it is important to engage in some introspection from time to time. It's good to be reminded that we are imperfect and can use some improvement. I challenge you to study the passage and then take a long look at your state of being. If there are improvements to be made, ask God to help you put them into action. Don't just recognize your faults and leave them as they are. Be a doer of the faith, not just a believer.

Love,

Kelli Raí

Praise and Glory

John 3:30 (NLT) "He must become greater and greater, and I must become less and less."

Hello Beautifuls,

Have you ever been moved to sing or speak in front of a group of people? Have you been moved to do an act of kindness for someone else? When everything is said and done, and we are left alone with our thoughts, we should consider the "why" of our actions. We should ask ourselves, "Am I driven to do things so that I can get the praise or am I driven to do things so that God can get the praise?"

John the Baptist was a peculiar man. He lived away from civilization, wore clothes made of animal skin, and ate locust, honey, and whatever else God provided for him in the wilderness. Yet, John was a mighty man of God who spoke truth. He did not want fame and fortune for himself; he was focused on God and the coming of the Messiah. John knew that his purpose was to be a light for God and to make a way for the Messiah to come into His ministry. After John baptized Jesus, people flocked to Jesus, many of whom were formerly followers of John the Baptist. John's disciples were alarmed and told him what was happening. His response was "... I am filled with joy at His success. He must become greater and greater, and I must become less and less."

In our culture, the thought is that we should push to get praise for ourselves; we should strive to be popular and have worldly success. God's way teaches us to do the opposite. We should do right because it is right, not for any accolades. Our drive and our purpose should be based on what God desires us to do. We are here to help each other get to Heaven. We must strive to help each other here on earth to make life a little easier for those who are having a difficult time.

I challenge you to go against the grain of the world and live for God. In whatever you do, give Him the praise. Live your life by being a light that guides someone to the Lord.

Love,

Kelli Raí

Exercise Faith

Mark 9:24 (NLT) "The father instantly cried out, 'I do believe but help me overcome my unbelief!'"

Hello Beautifuls,

In my life, when I go through especially rough periods, I find it difficult to apply the fundamental Christian belief of faith to my situations. This week, in particular, I had to recognize the fact that I do believe that Jesus can and will bring me through this trial, but I need Him to help my unbelief when I don't think He's moving fast enough. He said in His word that He would never leave or forsake me. (Heb. 13:5) He also said that He would supply all my needs (Phil 4:19) but it feels like this trial is just going on and on. At times it seems that God is too quiet. Doubt creeps in and I think that maybe everything I see in front of me is just too overwhelming. Selfishly, my concern is to just see a good result instead of going through the steps of relying on God for strength and guidance. But during trials, we must exercise our faith! If we cognitively believe that He is concerned about us and wants to save us, then we have to apply that faith to our hard times. When it seems too difficult to do that and my faith is weak, I have to use Mark 9:24 as a prayer. I also have to pray fervently and read His word.

When I do my part by studying His word and praying, my Heavenly Father does not stay silent. He communicates in different ways to let me know that He, indeed, has me in His hands. In worship this morning I read that if you are seeking direction, to study God's word to hear Him speak. (I hadn't studied God's word in the past two weeks, which was why He seemed silent.) I sent an email to some friends of mine asking them to pray for me and a friend sent this verse: 1Peter 5:10 (KJV) "But the God of all grace, who hath called us into his eternal glory by Christ Jesus, after that ye have suffered a little while, make you perfect, stablish, strengthen, settle *you*." This verse was confirmation that He is with me and that eventually He is going to settle me! This afternoon, I was driving home with my son Solomon and I asked him about homework. He told me that all he had to do was his spelling contract. I asked, "what about your memory verse? Do you know it?" He replied "Without faith no one can please God Hebrews 11:6." That was God telling me directly that in order to please Him, I must have faith!

I desire to please God; I also desire to be on the other side of this trial. In the midst of this trial, I am thankful that God loves me enough to communicate the fact that He has everything under control. He has taken the time to give me a soothing word so that I will stop stressing myself out about things I cannot control. I'm sharing this message with you to let you know that if He will do it for me, He will do it for you. We are His children. Seek His guidance, study His word, listen to what He has to say, and then follow His lead. We must have faith, not over just small things, but also over big things. Did He not create this entire universe from nothing? Then surely He can bring order to the chaos of your life. Our God can do anything. He knows all. Once again I am strong in my faith and I know that God is going to take care of ALL my needs.

I pray that your faith is increased.

Love,

Kelli Raí

Stay Close

1 Chronicles 7:22 (KJV) "And Ephraim their father mourned many days, and his brethren came to comfort him."
John 11:19 (KJV) "And many of the Jews came to Martha and Mary, to comfort them concerning their brother."
1 Thessalonians 4:16-18 (KJV) "For the Lord himself shall descend from Heaven with a shout, with the voice of the archangel, and with the trump of God: and the dead in Christ shall rise first: Then we which are alive and remain shall be caught up together with them in the clouds, to meet the Lord in the air: and so shall we ever be with the Lord. Wherefore comfort one another with these words."

Hello Beautifuls,

Have you ever felt lost, devastated, or discouraged because something terrible happened in your life? The closer we get to the last days of earth, the more we will experience life-changing events: death, natural disasters, financial ruin, failed relationships, etc. And in these times, we need to rally together to support and lift each other up.

We constantly hear about the "last days" but we rarely hear instruction about what we should do in those times besides "run to the hills." Here are my thoughts on what to do. When something terrible happens to us or to those close to us, we are to give a helping hand. We should comfort each other, help each other, lift each other up in prayer, and/or be present for each other.

Recently a large group of us lost a man who was a "giant for Jesus." It's still hard to believe that he's gone. And if we, his friends and acquaintances, feel this way, we can only imagine what his sisters, parents, extended family and close friends are going through.

In this time while we are all hurting, we must rally together and lift each other up. When I'm weak, be strong for me and when you're weak, I'll be strong for you. Even though at times we may not feel like it, we have to cling to God's promises. The major promise is that Jesus is coming back to get us and take us to Heaven. Then, after 1000 years in Heaven, we will inhabit the New Jerusalem and spend all of eternity together. Thank the LORD that we have something to look forward to!

Let's stay close to Jesus so that He can strengthen us in the hard times and give us power in the good times. Let's stay close to each other and keep each other encouraged.

Love,

Kelli Raí

Small Things

Isaiah 26:3 (NLT) "You will keep in perfect peace all who trust in you, all whose thoughts are fixed on you!"

Hello Beautifuls,

Very recently I had a conversation about how we can be attacked spiritually. Sometimes there are big things that rattle us and sometimes there are a series of small things that really get to us. That concept made so much sense to me! For a seasoned Christian, when one sees a big catastrophe occur in his or her life, it makes every bit of sense to run right to God. But when something seemingly small happens: a stupid argument about nothing with a significant other, a flat tire, locking the house keys in the house, hurt feelings, etc., running to God doesn't cross the mind. A series of small things can mount up and if you are not accustomed to going to God with big, small, and medium sized things – everything – you could become overwhelmed when you're being attacked with the small things!

Small things can become something humongous. I remember being told about Chinese water torture. It is a torture tactic in which water is slowly dripped onto a restrained prisoner's forehead over a period of time, which can drive the prisoner insane. This is just an example of how something so small and simple can turn into something big.

I've said all that to say, go to God with everything. Every little thing that comes your way, you should be in open communication with God about them. When you are in constant communication with God about things in your life, you should be able to see a situation for what it is a bit quicker and a bit better than if you try to constantly do things on your own. God is concerned about every aspect of your life. You should share with Him more.

My challenge to you is to make an effort to talk to God about the good things that happen as well as the bad things that happen no matter how big or small they seem to you.

Love,

Kelli Raí

He's Got You!

1 Peter 5:7 (NLT) "Give all your worries and cares to God, for he cares about you."

Hello Beautifuls,

On August 17, 2016, I was reminded that God cares about my cares. For some reason I was feeling very heavy in an emotional way and I could not shake it. I did not quite know why I felt the way I was feeling because there was so much on my mind. Since it was a Wednesday, I figured I'd go to prayer meeting: I don't usually go and I hoped that maybe it could help lighten my mood. I attended prayer meeting and appreciated the message and I did feel a bit lighter, but not completely. When I left church, I planned to go to the gas station then to the grocery store. Between the gas station and the grocery store, I learned, via text, that my Uncle Archie passed away. Confusion washed over me and I didn't know if I should still go to the store. My stern inner voice said, "Your life didn't stop. You still need to go to the store for fruit and vegetables."

When I walked into the store, I felt as if I was in a haze. As I "floated" through the produce, I heard someone call to me. It was Danny from church (who knew my dad while he was alive). We started talking and he testified to me about what he was going through and how he was holding on to faith. He expressed that the pastor's message was confirmation that he was doing what he needed to do. His testimony was exactly what I needed to hear! A phrase he used to describe how God assured Him gave me chills. "I got you!" That's exactly what God says to me when I worry about money! I almost cried. I told him, "God used the pastor to speak to you and He is now using you to speak to me." We both got chills. We hugged a couple times then went our separate ways. My heaviness was gone.

Sometimes the message you need to hear will come from something or someone you weren't quite expecting. God may take you all around the bend so that you will be at the place where He will finally meet your need. If we are willing to be transparent and open with one another, God can use us more often to help each other along life's path. We are not alone and our lives are not our own. God placed us in each other's life path for the reason of holding a hand, giving a push, giving a pull and/or giving an encouraging word.

My challenge to you is to be willing to be there for someone else: be kind, be helpful, and be encouraging.

Love,

Kelli Raí

Here We Go Again

Psalm 74: 20 (NLT) "Remember your covenant promises, for the land is full of darkness and violence!"

Hello Beautifuls,

Every so often, I come back to an issue that I have to contend with again. Perhaps it's because there's a lesson that I need to learn that I haven't yet learned. And when I find myself back in the same uncomfortable situation I tend to revel in negative feelings before I actually go to God for guidance. What do you do when you find yourself in an unfavorable situation that you've been in before? Do you wallow in your trouble? Do you become depressed and despondent? Do you call a friend before you call on Jesus?

Something that I should do before I consider anything else, is to whisper a prayer for help. After that, I need to remind myself of how God rescued me the last time. Time and again God has delivered me out of bad situations and He's seen me through countless rough patches. He absolutely has performed miracles on my behalf on many occasions. Once I've remembered his goodness, it would then be time to pray again but this time I would remind God of what He promised me and ask Him to show up for me again. Let Him know that I remember what He did for me before and ask Him to do it again. Ask for another miracle. Ask for deliverance again. Ask for Him to show up once more for me in my condition. I should repeat any of these steps as many times as I need to until I come out of my negative state.

I find myself questioning how God could come through for me when I'm not faithful to Him. The answer to that is in Lamentations 3:21-23 (NLT) "Yet I still dare to hope when I remember this: The faithful love of the Lord never ends! His mercies never cease. Great is his faithfulness; his mercies begin afresh each morning." I find myself wondering if I should keep asking God for the same thing over and over. The answer is in Luke 11:8-10 (NLT) "But I tell you this—though he won't do it for friendship's sake, if you keep on knocking long enough, he will get up and give you whatever you need because of your shameless persistence. And so I tell you, keep on asking, and you will receive what you ask for. Keep on seeking, and you will find. Keep on knocking and the door will be opened to you. For everyone who asks, receives. Everyone who seeks, finds. And to everyone who knocks, the door will be opened." (Read from verse 5 for context.)

It can be easy to think that God would treat us as harshly as perhaps we would treat others or ourselves. He is sovereign. He is our Father, Creator and Savior. He loves us and wants us to come to Him with all of our wants and needs, even if it's for the same thing again!

I challenge you to go to God first.

Love,

Kelli Raí

In a Quiet Voice

1 Kings 19:12 (NLT) "And after the earthquake there was a fire, but the Lord was not in the fire. And after the fire there was the sound of a gentle whisper."

Hello Beautifuls,

Have you ever had the experience of hearing God speak to you but only you could hear it? It wasn't a clap of thunder or a surround-sound rumble, but a quiet voice, and you just knew in your spirit that it was Him? In the bible, God speaks in a thunderous sound, a whirlwind, and also loud enough for all to hear as He did at Jesus' baptism (Luke 3:21). The bible tells us that He also speaks in a whisper, one on one, as described in 1 Kings 19:12.

God isn't always going to speak in a thunderous sound because not every situation calls for that. He will speak quietly just so you can hear it because what He has for you is just for you. Lately, I have felt a great amount of stress and anxiety, often for no reason at all. One evening, in the midst of feeling overwhelmed, God said to me very clearly, "that's not for you to worry about. You are okay. It is okay. It's not what you think." That message reassured me. I took some deep breaths and I calmed down. I was carefree until my anxiety resurfaced a few hours later. The message He gave to me was something that I had to hold on to in order to become calm once again.

Not only does He speak words of comfort, His still, small voice will also tell you to do something or not to do something. At the moment, you won't know why you should listen to the voice but the reason will either be revealed in time, or you will just have a knowing in your spirit that you did the right thing by being obedient. Whether you listen or ignore it, you may find yourself exclaiming, "something told me to do [or not to do] such and such!" You will be happy you adhered or disappointed that you did not believe it was important enough to follow the instructions. God cares about you so much, He speaks directly to you. He wants you to have awesome experiences with Him. He wants to save you. He wants to love you. He's interested in having a deep relationship with you, so He will talk to you and He yearns for you to listen. You are important to Him.

I challenge you to spend enough time in personal worship to recognize when God speaks to you. I challenge you to realize that you are so important to Him that He speaks to you all the time; you just need to listen.

Love,

Kelli Raí

Alarm Clock

Psalms 143:8 (NLT) *"Let me hear of your unfailing love each morning, for I am trusting you. Show me where to walk, for I give myself to you."*

Hello Beautifuls,

God literally woke me up this morning! I'm not just repeating the often-heard phrase "God woke me up this morning and started me on my way...." The only way my eyes popped open at the exact time I would have heard my second alarm was God gently awakening me with one of His love songs softly playing in my mind. My alarms didn't go off. The sound wasn't even working on my phone this morning. Believe me, I checked and powered my phone off then on again. (Sound worked after that. This has never happened to my phone before.) You could say that it was my body clock, but my body clock never wakes me up exactly when I should be awake. I know this was God being my alarm.

In the wake of my great disappointment with how the 2016 elections went, I am reminded that God is still concerned with my well being. He cares about things that I think are too small for His focus like waking up on time or being on time for work and school. I have said this before, "He cares about our cares!" No matter how small they seem, God cares about them. Do you know why He cares? It is because He created us and He loves us. He calls us His children. He calls us His friends. He wants to give us eternal life.

Even if situations don't seem to pan out exactly the way we wish they would, God is with us. He has a plan for our lives and we need to trust Him and look to Him for guidance. We should give ourselves to Him and listen to His voice. If He tells us to stand up and fight in a situation, that's what we should do. If He says to be still, prayerful and to be faithful, that's what we should do. If He tells us to stay the course and simply follow His lead, that's what we should do. He has allowed us to be alive at this time in history for a reason. He cares about the big things that happen to us as well as the small things we face each day.

I challenge you to keep putting your trust in Him; keep looking to Him.

Love,

Kelli Raí

He Will Show Up: He has Plans for You!

Jeremiah 1:5 (NLT) "I knew you before I formed you in your mother's womb. Before you were born, I set you apart and appointed you as my prophet to the nations."
Jeremiah 29:11, 12 (NLT) "For I know the plans I have for you," says the Lord. "They are plans for good and not for disaster, to give you a future and a hope. In those days when you pray, I will listen."

Hello Beautifuls,

Have you ever felt like you have been set up for failure? Even in situations where you know that God led you into the situation: that you surely were going to fail? I recently had the experience of feeling as if I'd gotten set up. I looked at my situation, hopelessly, as if God was just going to leave my family and me to suffer. And, even though I was and am sure that God has led me to this point, there is possibility of failure, through no fault of my own. Left up to me, I will not be successful, and I'll be bankrupt in the process.

Jeremiah reminds us all that God knew us BEFORE He formed us in our mother's womb and that He already had plans for us; "plans for good and not disaster" (Jeremiah 1:5; 29:11). With that reminder, I must remember that yes, He did guide me to this point and that He will show up and come through for me. His plans for me have far exceeded anything I could have ever imagined or hoped for, so He definitely will show up. I have to continue to trust and believe and ask and expect for Him to move on our behalf. Before I had the question, He had the answer, but I have to wait for Him to do what He's already planned to do.

I had a moment of despair. I am human and it is natural for us to have trouble with trusting God at times. In my moment, I sent a text to my brother to say a prayer for me right there and then. Without knowing my need, he said the perfect thing to God, and I just smiled. Then we had a conversation. After that, I looked at my situation closely and my mood improved one hundred percent! Even though I realized that things were out of my hands and that I had to wait on God, I was happy!

When you face a dilemma that is disheartening, how do you react? Do you get mad and throw up your hands? Do you pray? Do you go to God? Do you have friends intercede for you? Problems will always come as long as we keep living. It's how we deal with the event that makes the difference. God already knows what's up, so you should make it a point to talk to Him and rely on Him to help you through it. He has plans for you and He knows you better than you know yourself. Go to His word for reminders of His promises. Make it a point to develop friendships with people who love God and who will pray for you. Also, be willing to intercede for someone else, because whatever you're going through; trust that someone else is more than likely going through a worse situation than yours.

I challenge you to look beyond your situation and pray for someone else who may be going through. Watch how God works things out for you. Remember how He has come through for you in times past. Hold on to your faith!

Love,

Kelli Raí

When God Says "It's Time"

James 4:7, 8 (NLT) "So humble yourselves before God. Resist the devil, and he will flee from you. Come close to God, and God will come close to you. Wash your hands, you sinners; purify your hearts, for your loyalty is divided between God and the world."

Hello Beautifuls,

Sometimes when we ask God for something, we might imagine that He'll just snap His holy fingers and things will change just like that. While I believe that God has the power to do anything, including speaking a miracle and it happens, God usually does not work with us that way. If God acted like a fairy godfather, it would not do us very good. We would be spoiled little brats expecting everything to just happen for us in microwave seconds because we asked. It's important to believe in the power of God and that He can do anything, but when you ask for something, expect that, depending on the request, He may take you through a series of trials to shape you, humble you, and prepare you for greater things.

In October of 2014, I wrote a prayer list, and on that prayer list, I absentmindedly wrote: "be in a new house within a year." Little did I know that God put that in my mind to write down and little did I know at that time that the trials I faced the next year would be tied in to that prayer request. That one request alone was really asking God to grow me and prepare me for greater things with which He wanted to bless me. You may say to yourself, "it's just a house." But the idea is not just a house. I was asking God to enlarge my territory, but He would not enlarge my territory without humbling me and teaching me how to deal with more. I was asking God to take me to the next level. He would not do that without teaching me some very important lessons that would cause me take inventory of what was and was not important in my life.

God took to shaping my character that year. He held me in the fire for what seemed like way too long. When I wanted to give up, He reminded me that I was in His hands the whole time and that I would not be consumed by it, but that it would just change me and that I had asked Him to change me. He would send my brother friends and sister friends with reassurance and comfort so that I would remember Him. He woke me up with songs that helped me feel strong in Him. He sent me messages in sermons and devotionals as confirmation that He was with me and that He was busy changing my life. I clung to Him when my pain was most unbearable. I kept believing His power and that the hurtful parts of my trials would not last forever. And now, after the time of fire, He gave me what I asked for: a new house. He has enlarged my territory, literally!

This is not an opportunity for me to boast about material things, this is a testimony to relate that when God places something in your heart, if you are obedient and you trust Him, He will do His part. I am so blessed to have gone through every single thing that I went through, the highs and the lows, because God was with me and I had no doubt. I want you to know that He does not ever want us to become complacent. God wants us to be in tune with Him and ready to walk into the next chapter of our book when it's time.

He wants to have such a close relationship with Him that we will recognize His voice and His plan. If He says, "go back to school and finish your degree," trust that when you enroll, He will give you the strength to finish. I know for a fact, because enrolled in August of 2012 and graduated on May 15, 2016! If He tells you that He can heal your relationship, trust that He will but you have to be obedient, it's not always the other person who is at fault. If God says, "trust Me, I got you;" trust Him! He's got you!!! The day of the settlement meeting for the house, I was reminded of the words of the song "It's Time" by Kirk Franklin: "...and giving up feels wrong when you've been waiting for so long / for destiny and victory to finally collide / there's no sound more sweeter than when God says it's time...." It's an amazing feeling for something that you've longed for, which God placed in you, to finally come to fruition. God is so magnificent!

I challenge you today to begin to trust God again. If you already do, be willing to draw even closer to Him. He will draw closer to you. He loves you! He wants to be with you. He wants to bless you far beyond anything you have ever imagined.

Love,

Kelli Raí

Persevere

Philippians 3:13, 14 (NLT) "No, dear brothers and sisters, I have not achieved it, but I focus on this one thing: Forgetting the past and looking forward to what lies ahead, I press to reach the end of the race and receive the heavenly prize for which God, through Jesus Christ, is calling us."

Hello Beautifuls,

When things get hard for you, do you give up or do you stay at it until you get through it? One thing I have realized about myself is that my first instinct is to give up when things get to be too hard. But I have learned that it's not okay for me to do that. Giving up doesn't help the problem. I can step away from it and come back to it later, but I shouldn't totally give up on it (unless it's a toxic situation – then run!).

When I was finishing my degree online, there were semesters where it seemed that the course load would be too much for me to take 3 classes at a time while working full-time with a serious commute. Giving up was not an option because I had put so much into my higher education. Come to think of it, my husband had sacrificed, too, and my children had been affected. My parents had already paid for my education in the past and it was time for me to complete it. I couldn't allow myself give up. I had to push through it and get it done.

Knowing that my first instinct is to quit, God placed some pretty clear messages in a few devotionals I read during that time. The message: persevere. If He has set things in motion for me, He will be with me throughout the task. God doesn't give an assignment then walk away; He stays ever near to guide and protect and to be of comfort if things seem a bit much. He promised not to abandon us, and I believe him.

My challenge to you is to persevere. Whatever God has set in motion for you to accomplish, stay at it, even if it seems impossible. Remember, you're not doing this on your own; He is with you.

Love,

Kelli Raí

We All have Flaws

Romans 3:23, 24 (NLT) "For everyone has sinned; we all fall short of God's glorious standard. Yet God, in his grace, freely makes us right in his sight. He did this through Christ Jesus when he freed us from the penalty of our sins."

Hello Beautifuls,

I have to confess that I hate being wrong. I absolutely detest when I'm the one making the mistake. It seems to happen way too often for my liking and once the error has been made and I'm left to myself, I feel so low and remorseful. Truly, when I'm in that position I feel as if I'm in the bottom of a well, especially if I have hurt someone else.

My feelings about being wrong and causing others pain comes from the fact that for years, I always thought that I was right. It wasn't until the first real argument with my husband as a newlywed that I realized I wasn't perfect. That was a life-changing moment. (Smile) The jolt helped me look at myself more closely: listen to the things I say to the people I love, be aware of my tone, analyze my motives, be open to make changes if necessary, etc. Even though it helped me realize how far away I am from perfection, I still fail sometimes and find myself in a pit of sadness because of my actions.

The verse, Romans 3:23, is a reminder that we all have sinned. The fact we all fall short of what God wants for us should make me humble enough to ask for forgiveness and to do everything in my power to make things right. This logic should be applied in our relationship with God and our relationships with people. If you mess up, don't be afraid to ask for forgiveness, then make it right and try not to hurt that person again if you can help it. Learn from mistakes and try to be a better person when you come out of the uncomfortable situation.

Love,

Kelli Raí

Getting the "A"

Psalm 37:4, 5 (NLT) "Take delight in the Lord, and he will give you your heart's desires. Commit everything you do to the Lord, and he will give you your heart's desires."

Hello Beautifuls,

In the fall of 2012, I enrolled at University of Maryland University College. My husband, Brandon, encouraged me to go back to school to complete my Bachelor's degree, especially at that moment when I found myself unemployed, again. Through prayer for guidance, I chose my major (English) and minor (Psychology) and began the journey. This was a daunting challenge as I had not studied in school since the late 90s and I didn't know that I had the energy, patience, and stamina to delve into studying and trying to get good grades again. And also, this was a new concept: online classes. God's presence, guidance, and help were ever with me.

In October of 2013, I was hired by Takoma Academy part time with the vision of my position becoming full time at the end of the school year. God made it so that my job became full time, which was a blessing, but my classes at UMUC were far from over. This posed a new challenge: take classes while working full time, with a commute on top of that. Realizing that the kind of time I had when employed part time, I would not have this semester, I prayed for A's (just like the kids do) in the two classes I took. Guess what? I got A's in both classes. And I know without a doubt that I did not deserve an A in one of the classes, but God heard my prayer and decided to say yes to me. I am SO glad!

When we do as the verse says and "commit everything [we] do to the Lord, he will give [us] our heart's desires." I've said it before: He cares about our cares. Is receiving an A in a college course a big deal? Probably not in the scheme of things, however it means something to me. I aim to be an example for my children who will be in college before I know it. I want them to do their best and while doing their best, rely on God to take them to wherever they are supposed to be. I can't only rely on own wit, God has to step in and do what I can't begin to do, because He sees what I can't see.

I challenge you to commit everything you do to the Lord and watch how He works it all out for you.

Love,

Kelli Raí

Works Cited

Scriptures quoted from KJV are from the Holy Bible, King James Version, Crown copyright © in UK.

Scriptures quoted from NIV are from the HOLY BIBLE, NEW INTERNATIONAL VERSION ®, copyright © 1973, 1978, 1984, 2011 by Biblica, Inc. ® Used by permission. All rights reserved worldwide.

Scriptures taken from the HOLY BIBLE, NEW INTERNATIONAL READER'S VERSION®. Copyright © 1995, 1996, 1998 by International Bible Society. Used by permission of Zondervan Publishing House. All rights reserved.

Scriptures quoted from the NKJV are taken from the Holy Bible, New King James Version, copyright © 1982 by Thomas Nelson, Inc. All rights reserved.

Scripture quotations marked NLT are taken from the Holy Bible, New Living Translation, copyright © 1996, 2004. Used by permission of Tyndale house Publishers, Inc., Wheaton Illinois 60189. All rights reserved.

Adams, Roy. "The Mystery of His Deity." Adult Sabbath School Bible Study Guide: The Wonder of Jesus, 6 April 2008, Pacific Press Publishing Association, Idaho.

Anthony Brown & group therAPy. "And You Never Will." *Everyday Jesus*, Tyscot Music & Entertainment. 2015.

Maurette Brown Clark. "It Ain't Over." *The Dream*, Atlanta International Records, Inc. 2006.

Dorinda Clark-Cole. "Nobody But God." *Live From Houston – The Rose Of Gospel*, Gospocentric Records. 2008

James Cleveland And The Southern California Community Choir. "Give It To Me." Savoy Records. 1976.

Kirk Franklin. "It's Time." *Losing My Religion*, Fo Yo Soul Recordings, RCA Records. 2015.

Donald Lawrence & The Tri-City Singers. "Encourage Yourself." *Finale: Act II*, EMI Gospel. 2006.

Marvin Sapp. "You Are God Alone." *Diary of a Psalmist,* Verity Records. 2003.

Tye Tribbett & G.A. "Answer." *Life*, Sony Music Entertainment Inc. 2004.

Tye Tribbett & G.A. "Sinking." *Victory Live,* Columbia Records. 2006.

Hezekiah Walker & The Love Fellowship Crusade Choir. "Second Chance." *The Essential Hezekiah Walker,* Zomba Recording LLC. 2007

Kirk Whalum. "Falling in Love with Jesus." *The Gospel According to Jazz: Chapter 2,* Word Entertainment. 2002.

Justin A. Wilson. "No Room." *A Wilson & Company Christmas,* Breath Of Life Records, LLC. 2011

DeWayne Woods. "Let Go." *Introducing DeWayne Woods & When Singers Meet,* Zomba Recording LLC. 2006.

29827082R00070

Made in the USA
Columbia, SC
24 October 2018